LIVING

—— IN THE ——

FLOW

A GUIDE TO DISCOVERING YOUR
PURPOSE AND VALUE
IN THIS WORLD

JEANINE
SCIACCA

BALBOA
PRESS

A DIVISION OF HAY HOUSE

Balboa Press books may be ordered through booksellers or by contacting:

Balboa Press
A Division of Hay House
1663 Liberty Drive
Bloomington, IN 47403
www.balboapress.com.au
1 (877) 407-4847

Print information available on the last page.

ISBN: 978-1-5043-1627-9 (sc)
ISBN: 978-1-5043-1628-6 (e)

Balboa Press rev. date: 02/07/2019

CONTENTS

ACKNOWLEDGEMENTS

An exceptionally special thanks to Almighty God, from whom all things come, including the chapters of this book, and all the thoughts, ideas, people, and guidance that made it all possible.

My deepest, heartfelt thanks to Dezy, for your unwavering and loving support of everything I am and do. You have been a pillar of strength always and have never let me down. God has blessed me with you in my life. I love you and always will.

A special thanks to my mother, who repeatedly told me from a very young age that I can be or do anything. She instilled in me the confidence and the belief in myself that has shaped me into the woman I am today. I would also like to thank her for her tireless effort in proofreading my manuscript.

A special thanks to my father, who taught me to appreciate and have a sense of awe for the hand of God in all living and nonliving creations.

I love you both eternally.

A very special thanks also to the late José Silva, for his wonderful work and creating the Silva Method, a personal development programme that not only changed my life but offered me the opportunity to teach it to others, which is now a key part of my business.

Thanks to John Maxwell, the John Maxwell team, the faculty, and the members who inspired me and gave me the most wonderful support and training in the transition from my corporate life to following my dream.

This book is dedicated to my beloved late brother, Gianmarco Sciacca, who blessed my life in his extraordinary twenty-one years living on earth and even more so with his passing. His passing was a divine intervention that had the greatest impact on my life. I love you and thank you for the angel that you are.

INTRODUCTION

Writing a book was never my intention or something I aspired to do. However, one night while lying in bed, a few hours after falling asleep, about midnight, I was in a lucid dream state and started praying. I asked God, "What is my next best step for my life?"

Totally surprised, I received an answer as clear as a voice talking to me that said, "Write your book."

Doubting the clear and swift answer I received, I started negotiating with more questions. The dialogue in my mind went something like this:

Me: Write a book?

God: Yes.

Me: What book?

God: How can you help people beyond your physical presence?

Me: Wow! Okay. I see, with a book. What's the book about?

God: How can you help people beyond your physical presence? What do you want people to know? What do you want people to do?

Me: Yes, okay, I get that, but what's the book about?

God: What do you want people to know? What do you want people to do? Stay with that question, and everything will come to you.

I lay there in bed, in the dark with my eyes closed, in a half-awake, half-asleep state. Without effort, my mind started to wander, and in no time, the thing I wanted people to know, above all else, is what their highest priorities *really* are. Three things stood out for me, which are the importance of developing an awareness of our constant connection with Source (which I call God), finding our life's purpose, and developing our intuition to guide us.

In this dream state, my mind drew three circles, like bubbles, each with one of these priorities in them. They then merged to form a Venn diagram, and as the circles overlapped, every segment that was a combination of any of these priorities popped with clear, vivid titles. The centre point is the result of living with all three priorities active in one's life, which is, in my view, living in the flow. My mind then wandered to the purpose of us being alive and asking the question, "Why we are here in the first place? What's it all about?" This question made me realise that living our highest priorities is only the first part, because living with a purpose is about serving others, which led my mind to ponder about Part 2 of this book.

I started to drift in and out of sleep at this point but wanted to capture this download I just received. Have you ever had a dream and, as you woke up and opened your eyes, it disappeared? I was concerned that if I opened my eyes and put on the light to make notes, this dream or vision would dissolve. To be sure this wouldn't happen, I ran it over and over in my mind and prayed that it would not dissipate when I got up and put the light on. I then did just that and scribbled it all down in just a few minutes and went back to sleep.

The next morning, I woke up with a vague recollection of jotting down some notes about a book I believed I'd been guided to write.

I referred to the scribbled notes I wrote down the night before, and with amazement, I realised I had an outline of the entire book, right there. Every chapter. I just had to write the chapters out in full.

This book is the result of honouring what was supposedly asked of me, because of the answer to the question I asked of God, who clearly answered. I am so grateful for the guidance and inspiration to share this with you, and my wish is that this book adds value to your life; I hope it's simple and easy to follow, and more than that, it is my wish that you apply this in *your* life. Why? So that your life can get better and better over time, with the intention that you live your best life and, in doing so, inspire others to do the same. May Almighty God bless you always, and may this book be a close companion that you can refer to often, like a friend.

PART 1

Your Highest Priority

I'm sure you've heard the expression by Woody Allen, "If you want to make God laugh, tell him your plans." I wondered what that meant for many years. I now understand it a lot better. Our plans, when looking at them from a bigger picture perspective, are often so trivial, self-indulgent, and ambitious and there to satisfy us in the short term, until we very quickly have a new desire that becomes our focus. I was like this myself and am speaking from my own humble experience.

Gratefully, I've matured somewhat and have a deeper understanding that I wish to share with you, which is all about the three key areas that I call your highest priorities. Why? Why the highest priorities? It is my unassuming belief that these priorities, when applied, integrated, and embraced into our hearts and at the core of who we truly are, as well as implemented into our lives, give us the keys to eternal satisfaction, peace, joy, harmony, and bliss that no material possession or worldly plan can ever satiate. These are the three priorities for a fulfilling and meaningful life:

1. Developing a consistent connection to Source energy
2. Finding your life's purpose
3. Developing and refining your intuition

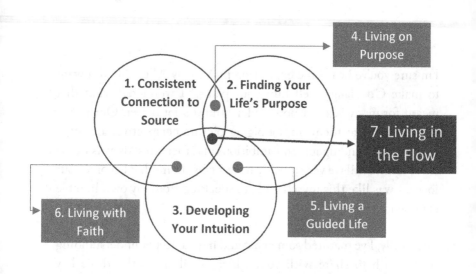

CHAPTER 1

Developing a Consistent Connection to Source Energy

I started this book with the first chapter about developing a consistent connection to Source energy, not because I think it's the most important or the first step to living in the flow, but more to create the awareness that it is from Source energy that *all* things come. There is only one universal Source from where all things come. *All* things. Once you have an awareness that you don't even take a breath on your own, you don't beat your heart yourself, or digest your own food (consciously), or filter your blood, or think a thought without this one universal Source energy acting and flowing through you. When you can appreciate that every breath you take is from Source energy, you'll have an awakening that has the potential to change your life forever, in the most beautiful and profound way.

You and I cannot lift a finger without Source energy. It is the very essence of all life and all non-living things too. Ask yourself: Who shines the sun? Who lights the fireflies? Who turns the earth? Who creates the music? What is love? Who grows the baby in the womb? It is such a complex miracle of creation from literally no form, a single drop of protoplasm, to an incredibly complex form. How is it possible that the sun is the centre of our solar system and all planets revolve around the sun, specifically our beautiful planet, that if only one centimetre closer to the sun would burn, or one centimetre farther away would freeze. What is arranging this all in such perfection?

Where does the perfume of a flower come from, if they grow in dirt that has no perfume? Where and *how* does the colour and creamy texture of an avocado get created out of brown soil or the colour and texture of a banana, or the white crisp cauliflower? How does it grow perfectly every time? And how do all these colours and textures and flavours get created out of brown soil that has none of these qualities?

How does a complex creation like a bird with feathers, a beak, eyes, feet, nails; a digestive, reproductive, respiratory, circulatory, and nervous system; and so much more get created out of liquid inside a shell? There are no pipes attached, no life support system, no cord, and no supply of all these components. It is on its own inside a shell. How is this created?

How does a butterfly emerge, with beautiful coloured wings and an intricately designed body with eyes, legs, reproductive system, magnificent wings with colourful designs, a respiratory system, and so on, get formed out of liquid? Yes, it is liquid in the cocoon that resulted from a decomposing caterpillar. How does this get created? And more impressive is that the DNA of the butterfly is different from the DNA of the caterpillar. How is this created?

My father is a doctor of geology and appreciates nature so much. He believes in creationism and dislikes all theories of evolution. He shared some interesting facts with me that amplified my sense of awe at nature's miracles. As an example, the Siberian salamander (*salamandrella keyserlingii*) is a little amphibian that defies all natural laws. They live in the north of Asia, close to the Arctic Circle and on permafrost plains, and they are known to survive deep freezes, as low as -45°. They can remain frozen for years (as dead) and upon thawing, they walk off. As my father says, it is incomprehensible if you do not believe that God can work and create in the realm of the impossible and beyond our known physical laws.

Concerning the sciences (physics, chemistry, mathematics), millions of people still think that the human mind invented them and their laws. How far from the truth. No one ever invented anything. It was there to be discovered and understood. With regards to geology, my father learned to view rocks as live entities and accept that they are ever changing physically and chemically. For example, crystals in voids grow in different directions and against gravity all the time; having a food supply or the right chemical minerals brought to them via fluids (geodes as an example). And they start from zero, no seed. How were these created? Have you ever pondered this thought? They have identities, classes, and groups, very intelligently organised. Others change identities or chemistry with the changing of heat and pressure, for example, diamonds. Everything was there. How are they created?

If you contemplate creation in nature, a simple blade of grass, a flower, a tree, or a beautiful and intelligent animal like an elephant or dolphin, then have you even considered what a miracle of creation you are? You are the most complex creation in this universe. Where did you come from? Don't say your parents; their human bodies provided the droplet of protoplasm, but where did you come from? How were you created? All this divine intelligence that exists everywhere, including your eyes, reading this because light, in its perfection, reflects off the page, through your eyes, and gets interpreted by your brain because several neurons are firing (all without your effort or control) so that you are not only able to see these words but interpret them too. What a miracle of creation you truly are.

Have you ever contemplated your heart? In 2016, scientists at Waterloo University proved that emotions come from the heart and not from the mind. Individuals whose heart rate experienced wider variations displayed more wisdom and less bias-judgements. The heart is the centre of our life; you can continue living with a dead brain, but not with a dead heart. Your heart starts to beat only three weeks after conception, when you were the size of a mere poppy seed. Think of it. Think how small a poppy seed is. The heart works continuously for many years, with an average beating of one hundred thousand beats per day and over a period of seventy to ninety years. Your heart, the size of your fist, will pump more than a million barrels of blood, enough to fill up three long-range oil tankers. It has extreme precision and accuracy (to pale any Omega watch). It overruns and overrules your nervous system. You can anaesthetise your brain, nerves, and muscles, but not your heart. You cannot control it; your heart intelligently decides what your heart rate should be at any given moment, not you. It has its own internal power source and a unique electrical impulse that makes the muscle contract.

Try now, quickly, to squeeze your hand into a fist and then open it back again, over and over at the rate of seventy times per minute. Try! And notice how long you manage before your hand and arm muscles are tired, sore, and perhaps in spasm. You will not be able to withstand an hour, never mind a day and even less a year. How come your heart can? What kind of muscle is it? Isn't it still flesh, like the rest of your body? Do not try to explain the inexplicable. With humility and awe, we can appreciate that God gave us a heart and keeps it beating. We truly are nothing, we can do nothing, we cannot lift a finger, and we cannot breathe a breath without this almighty infinite power.

When you develop a constant awareness of this universal Source energy (and yes, it is something you intentionally develop), whether it is called God, infinite intelligence, or any other name, you start opening up a connection with this infinite power. This is why I started the book with this chapter.

When you intentionally develop a connection and awareness that everything lives and breathes, moves and vibrates, exists and changes form, gets created, or withers and dies because of this universal Source energy, you begin to see life as one big miracle, and you are in the centre of your miraculous life.

This awareness of Source energy is like a conduit, a connection between your consciousness and Source energy that is you. You are a physical extension of Source energy. Source is infinite, consistent, and ever present. You, on the other hand, can divert your attention away from or towards this one universal Source. This is your free will.

When you use the will, which is a faculty of the mind, to develop your awareness of Source energy and an awareness that it is from where all things come, you now have the benefit of tapping into this Source and literally develop, not just a relationship with Source, but a dependence on Source guiding your life, as it guides and perfectly organises this entire universe.

You can live unconsciously, or you can live consciously aware of the presence of Source energy everywhere. This is where your free will comes in.

I'm here to suggest to you that developing what I call Source energy consciousness is a necessary requirement to living a fulfilling, meaningful, happy, purposefully guided life that will direct you effortlessly to living a life beyond your wildest dreams, as you become the grandest version of yourself and truly make a difference in this world.

If you yearn to live a more fulfilling and creative life of love, happiness, and meaning, then it is your highest priority to firstly develop a consistent connection to Source energy and a constant awareness of this infinite Source from where all things come.

Ways to Develop a Constant Connection to Source Energy

- Keep a gratitude journal and write in it every single day. Consider the things people take for granted, like seeing colour. Imagine living in a black-and-white world. Be thankful for all five of your senses. Appreciate how good life is because of your senses. When you become grateful for every breath you take, you are well on your way to developing a consistent connection with Source. It's not extreme or exaggerated because the truth is, without Source energy, you don't have breath, and without breath, you no longer have this physical body, enjoying this wonderful gift of a human life experience.

Gratitude journaling should include as much as you can remember about what you have and what you get to do; you can choose how you want to be. You are not a victim; you create your own reality with your thoughts and feelings about any subject. Your attitude or viewpoint is your point of power, your choice. Remember: You are living in a universe of attraction. You get what you think about, whether you want it or not. The law of attraction is always in play and does not depend on your belief in it. Likewise, the law of gravity does not depend on your belief in or acceptance of it; it is the law.

Also list things that don't work out for you, that disappoint or hurt you, because without them, you would not be able to refine your wants, desires, and dreams. Bad times and negative situations can also be your greatest teachers, as long as you take responsibility for learning from them. By taking responsibility for your own happiness and unhappiness, you increase the desire to fulfil your dreams, so always be grateful for bad experiences and ask, what can this teach me? Or what can I learn from this situation? Journal that too.

Experience is not your greatest teacher; evaluated experience is. Be grateful for every lesson.

- Take nature walks and spend time in nature, slowly and silently; this allows the greatest observation of infinite miracles happening all at once, all around us. Notice everything from a tiny new life form growing out the ground, to a little bee doing its job intelligently, tirelessly, and diligently, collecting pollen from some miraculously and beautifully created perfect flower, and just ask yourself repeatedly, how was this created? *How* was this created? How was *this* created? How was this *created*?

  Watch birds fly and wonder to yourself how that magnificent creature was created to fly. From no form to a complex, beautiful, and perfect form, each species unique, each with its own colour and individual bird song. Take any flower and study it for several minutes, asking, how was this created? The infinite intelligence that exists everywhere is mind boggling. How does a strong and gigantic tree get created from a tiny seed? How? This whole planet is thriving and bursting with intelligent life, some so small we can't see it without a microscope, intelligent nonetheless. Some life is so complex, you cannot even fathom how it works, like your incredible brain, with powers and potential that are literally unlimited.

- Another way to develop a constant connection to Source energy is to pray. I am a person of faith, so if you're not, feel free to skip this part. Prayer is an intentional act. It is a wilful act of connecting with Source energy, and the more you practice it, the more you feel connected to this amazing Source and develop a real relationship that resembles an ongoing, loving, and supportive dialogue, similar to that with a special friend. I'm not here to teach anyone how to pray; however, I have found miracles show up more and more in my life when my prayer acknowledges that I'm a humble child of God, like everybody else; I actually use those words to keep me grounded, humble, and aware that everything I have, do, or am comes from this one universal Source. Everything in life is given *to* me, and I am grateful for it. No matter what prayer I pray, every day I include these words: "I am your humble child, I surrender; please guide my life so that I may fulfil my highest dharma [purpose]." With just that simple request, you summon this infinite Source to literally guide your life, which will always be one of beauty, purpose, and fulfilment that fills a need that *only* you can fill, in order to make this world a better place. This is living your best life.

• Meditation is another way to develop a consistent connection to Source energy. There are an infinite number of ways to meditate, and I'm not here to prescribe any particular one over another. However, the one element that is a focus, whether big or small, in any meditation, is the breath. With awareness and being intentional, you can remind yourself that every breath is given to you. It is not yours. You do not create it; you do not consciously breathe all day (otherwise, you would stop breathing if you forgot about it or when you sleep). It is humbling to be aware that every breath is from Source energy, which is guiding your breathing, living experience. This is because every breath, *every* single breath, is a gift in this human experience. It is not a given. Therefore, if you meditate, no matter the type of meditation, have an awareness that this breath that you can regulate, or slow down, or focus on, is a gift. It is literally a tangible experience of Source energy within you, as you breathe, keeping you alive. Wow. Isn't that wonderful?

Imagine what else this infinite Source can give you, if you ask for it with awareness that this is where all things come from, from the food you eat, to the body you feed, to the metabolism that keeps your blood warm. Everything, every thing, every single thing comes from this one universal Source energy.

Life *is* beautiful; see it everywhere.

CHAPTER 2

Finding Your Life's Purpose

Do you know your life's purpose? If you've answered no to this question, you're not alone. When I ask audiences this question, about 90 percent of them do not know their life's purpose.

This has got to be one of the big mysteries and frustrations for many people. I speak for myself here. My whole life, I never knew what I wanted to do with my life, let alone understand my life *purpose*. Whenever I heard anyone speak about life purpose, I actually got a bit annoyed, because I didn't even understand what that meant, for me.

What I did know was that I was mostly grateful for where my life was but not satisfied. Does that sound familiar? I've changed careers several times. I started off as a chef in the food service industry and then worked in supermarket retail for six years, after which time I left the retail side to join the supply side. After seven years and several roles, I immigrated to Australia and got into market research. All this time, for twenty years, I loved what I was doing. I loved learning new skills and new industries, and I had a successful career. However, I always had this gnawing thought in my head: *There's got to be more to life than this.*

If you've ever felt that way, I have good news: It doesn't have to stay that way. Finding your life's purpose is not as elusive as you think. If you have a true desire to know your life's purpose, with a few simple ideas and techniques, you too may find the thing that gives your life meaning. It fills your heart to the brim with an unquenchable desire to keep doing what you're doing because it lights your fire, it makes your heart beat faster, it gets you out of bed with a spring in your step each day, and it gives you lots of energy to handle whatever is in front of you with enthusiasm, courage, and inspiration.

The good news is, if you're looking to find your life purpose, you can learn from others who are sharing insights on the subject, which means you'll discover your purpose proactively. This is the best way. They say clever people learn from their mistakes, but wise people learn from other people's mistakes.

Like many people, I came to the decision to find my life's purpose as a result of a major event. This is what I call a cosmic slap. A cosmic slap is designed to wake you up. This does not necessarily have to be your experience.

It was Napoleon Hill who once said, "Within every temporary defeat lies the seed of an equivalent advantage." So here's my story:

In 2012, on July 4, my younger brother, Gianmarco Sciacca, passed on suddenly; he drowned, after suffering an epileptic fit whilst cleaning the garden around the pool. He was twenty-one years old.

This tragedy was the most devastating and heartbreaking experience of my life. It felt like my heart was ripped out of my chest; the pain inside was more than emotional. It was physical. Nothing had ever hurt so much and so deep. It left so many questions in my mind: *Why? Why him? Why so young? What's it all about?* However, the most valuable question that arose for me was, What if it was me? Yes, me. What if I passed on today; would I have any regrets? Am I happy with my own life? For the first time in my life, I sat with this question for days whilst in mourning, until I was honest with myself and realised that I was successful, but not fulfilled. I still felt that there had to be more to life than this. I suffered from what I term unfulfilling success. Gianmarco's passing brought me to a crossroads in my life, quickly and unforgivingly. I was earning good money, living in a comfortable home, with a loving partner, family, all the material possessions I needed and wanted; however, I was left unfulfilled, often stressed and overworked, living for another pay cheque or recognition from the company (I'm not sure which), and working way too many hours a day.

It was one thing admitting to myself I hadn't really lived my dream life, but it was a whole other thing knowing *what* to change, what to do, or how to go about finding the thing that would make me feel fulfilled. What I did know was that my calendar was full, week in and week out, with meetings and more meetings dealing with other people's agendas, whilst I was struggling to find time to do my own job, which often left me working after hours and weekends, just to be the hero and keep smashing my sales targets for recognition or a promotion. What was I thinking? Where was my life? Five years had flown by in this role, and it was not going to change unless I changed something.

Several years before, I used a personal development programme called the Silva Method, which helped me overcome some very challenging situations I was facing in my corporate job. Part of the Silva Method's training is developing your intuition. So a few months after my brother passed on, I got this intuitive feeling, this guided feeling, like a hunch, to join the John Maxwell Team (JMT). It is a global team of speakers, trainers, and coaches who are certified and trained by the world's No. 1 leadership guru, John Maxwell.

When I did join, I was blessed to have a mentor come into my life who had me on weekly mentorship calls. One night, he was talking about life purpose. I leaned in, hoping to find the answer to this enigma that had me frustrated for so long. What he shared changed my life.

He said, "Don't ask the question, what is your life's purpose? Ask the question, what are you *passionate* about? What makes your heart sing? Or what makes you cry, you are so passionate about it? Because in your passion lies your God-given purpose."

Well, that stuck with me and turned my reticular activation system (RAS) on full dial. My radar was on 24/7, searching for what I am passionate about. I am Italian, so I'm passionate just about everything: food, dancing, debating, music, art, photography, presenting, being intimate, good coffee, you name it, but that wouldn't be my life purpose. Nonetheless, I was more aware of my passions from that day onwards.

In the months that followed, after joining the JMT, I had learned so much about leadership and had grown personally and professionally, more than I had grown in many years, and I just wanted to share this with everybody, to help them the way it helped me. So I decided to book a large training room at work and offer a leadership presentation during lunchtime to anyone who was interested. I prepared the presentation with all my heart because I loved the content, and more than that, I loved the idea of helping others be more successful.

To my surprise, fourteen people showed up. At the end, I told the audience that if they liked what I shared in those forty-five minutes and wanted to learn more, I was offering a free twelve-week leadership course that would be held after hours (I didn't want to take people away from their day jobs). This was self-development, so an investment of their time. To my surprise, all fourteen people put their names down. I wasn't sure if anyone would sign up, but when you're on the right track in life, the universe paves the way forward. This was a sign to keep moving in this direction.

After delivering my very first leadership workshop, I was talking with a colleague at work. When she asked me how I enjoyed giving that presentation on leadership, I answered, "I loved it. I loved it with a passion."

As I said those words, it felt as though time stood still. I got goose bumps from head to toe, and I heard the voice of my mentor in my head: *In your passion lies your God-given purpose.*

I realised I was onto something that excited me beyond words and scared the you-know-what out of me at the same time.

In my heart, I knew that day was the best experience I had *ever* had at work. I cannot explain why or what, but it felt so good, and I felt so alive. I wasn't asked by anyone to do it. It wasn't work related, and it was my own presentation on leadership that (I was told) was inspiring, motivating, and refreshing. As I was still on my way to becoming fully certified by John Maxwell, which would entail travelling to the United States for a week, limiting beliefs started flooding in about not being credible as a leadership trainer, speaker, or coach because I had no prior experience to make this a career. Even so, the idea and the feeling did not leave me. It was there calling me, like a vocation (from the word *vocari*, that to which you are drawn, or that to which you are called).

The more I thought about this thing that I was passionate about, the more the voice in my head was holding me back with doubt, fear, and indecision. *You can't do that; don't be silly. Who would hire you, anyway? What credentials do you have in this space? What's your track record in training or speaking? How will you pay your bills and meet your monthly expenses? You'll never earn enough money; you'll go backwards in life in pursuit of this crazy idea you love so much. Okay, so you'll have such fun and be helping others, but you'll be worse off financially. Are you prepared to go backwards? Who knows how many years it will take to become an expert in this highly competitive field of speaking, training and coaching?*

So I started negotiating with my dream. Maybe I could become a trainer in my corporate job. A part of me felt sick with that idea. I thought to myself, *I don't want to train their content. I don't want to dance to someone else's tune, and I don't want to help just these people. I want to help as many people as I can.*

So now I was faced with a choice. Do I stay in my corporate job with all the security and comfort, or do I take this leap of faith and do what I'm really passionate about?

My heart knew what my passion was. My head was holding me in a prison with all these limiting beliefs. A few months later, I went to Orlando to get certified by John Maxwell; until I spent a week with John and his team of other speakers, trainers, and coaches, I could not see a way out of where I was, to where I wanted to end up. When I attended that particular event, my world opened up. Hundreds of other people were living my dream. They were all speakers, trainers, and coaches, adding value to others. I said to myself, *If they can do it, I can do it.* But how? I heard other people's stories, and they all inspired me; however, I still didn't know *how* I was going to do this.

I then remembered how the Silva Method helped me overcome my biggest challenges a few years prior, where I went from a place of being afraid of being fired at work, to becoming the top salesperson in the company, three years in a row. So on the flight back from Orlando to Sydney, I decided to do whatever it took to work on myself and my limiting beliefs; somehow, someway, I was going to live my dream life too and become a speaker, trainer, and coach.

Nonetheless, the one thing that gave me more courage, more than anything else, was my younger brother Gianmarco and his life quote, which was, "If you don't leap for what you want, how will you ever reach what you need?"

I copied those words onto his photograph, put it on my vision board, and looked at it every single day, and that gave me the courage to follow my dream. I kept telling myself to take one more step, any step, but keep moving forward. I registered a business name. I opened a business bank account. I continued to offer free Masterminds classes, one after the other, whilst in my corporate job. I joined Toastmasters and spoke about leadership every chance I got. In less than four months, a fellow Toastmaster asked me to speak at their annual conference and do a talk on leadership. I was gobsmacked. Me? And they offered to pay me fifteen hundred dollars for two twenty-minute speeches. At the time, with a lower awareness, I thought I was a winner to get a paid speaking gig. Looking back now, with higher awareness, I realise it was a sign from the universe that I was on the right track and moving towards living my life purpose.

The spell was broken. Which spell? The limiting belief that nobody would hire me as a credible resource and would not be able to make enough money. These limiting beliefs were just that: beliefs. The good news is, we can change our beliefs. All of us, including you. Once I realised this was the universe rewarding me, opening doors for me, guiding me, supporting me, encouraging me, and showing me what's possible, I had the confidence and courage to continue pursuing my dream of speaking, training and coaching. It gave me more faith in myself and in my dream.

In the months that followed, if I ever felt unsure or despondent, I would repeat in my head like a mantra, "Do what you can, with what you've got, from where you are." Take one more step and keep moving forward. I continued to do more of what I was doing. I did more Lunch 'n Learn free talks. I did twelve-week Mastermind classes. I did one, I did two, I did three. I started teaching leadership and doing Lunch 'n Learns and offering Mastermind classes across all divisions of the company. I even did them at night, Skyping with companies in South Africa. This created so much momentum that I earned the reputation of a leader who actively develops other leaders, and this coupled with my consistently ahead-of-target sales results got me promoted to director.

My friends and family congratulated me and said, "Jeanine, you must be so happy; you've achieved your dream."

It may have seemed like that to them because during my twenty years in corporate, I aspired to becoming a director. Why? I cannot say, except it was probably my ego believing that status was a sign of success, and that in some way it meant that all the years of hard work and experience paid off.

However, to me, I had not reached my dream; I had changed. Titles at this time of my life meant nothing to me. It was how I spent my time that mattered most. After doing all those Lunch 'n Learn presentations and Mastermind classes and teaching leadership and personal development, I was more convinced than ever that I wanted to leave the corporate world and add value to others in a significant way, making a difference. When you find your purpose, decisions become clearer. Value is not about money or titles; it is about creating value and adding value to others. Nothing else can be a substitute for that fulfilling purpose.

Six weeks after being promoted to director, I resigned from my corporate job to follow my dream. The years that followed have been the happiest and most fulfilling years of my entire life. I love the sense of freedom; I'm blessed enough to have had the most successful years emotionally, mentally, physically, financially, and spiritually, and it keeps getting better and better.

I had finally crashed through my proverbial fear barrier into my freedom and have never looked back.

You will always face a fear barrier when you consider taking action towards a higher ideal, a better life, or a bigger goal. Here's why:

If you want different results in your life, you must change your paradigm. Your results reflect your paradigm. If you alter your paradigm, you change your results. Results have always been determined by the paradigm. We all have an imaginary barrier between where we are and where we want to be. That's called our terror barrier. On the other side of the terror barrier is freedom. The terror barrier is just outside your comfort zone; it's the point where you are subject to a flow of negative, unhealthy emotions that you experience in that instant. There's a great feeling of dread and feeling of certainty, the feeling that you are doomed, which happens in an instant, when you think of doing something that you are scared of doing, even if you want to do it.

It is an automatic response in your body, even if you think it's safe intellectually. Your body experiences this terrible feeling of anxiety that convinces you the last thing in the world you want to do is actually take that step. Whenever people attempt to step outside their comfort zone, they go through four stages. They go from comfort to reason, to terror, to freedom. From comfort (I'm happy where I am), to reason (actually, I want more than this), to terror (oh my goodness, I can't do it; I'm not good enough), to freedom (oh, I actually *can* do it ... wow).

Most people never get past the terror stage; they just cycle round the first three stages.

The emotion appears to stem from the activating event, that is, whatever it is you are thinking of doing. The activating event doesn't have to be an act; it can be a feeling or a thought, and the thought can be real or imagined. Your body's response is the same, either way. You first get a thought of doubt, followed by an emotion of fear, which is expressed through your body as anxiety. The key thing to understand is that your body doesn't respond directly to the activating event; it responds to your *belief* about the activating event. Consider that your comfortable conditioning is made up of a mass of beliefs. By understanding the process, you can observe what's happening and in what order, because it's *understanding* that's a key part of the power to move forward, despite the feeling.

Very few people get through that terror barrier. It's rather unfortunate. Freedom is available to everyone. There isn't anyone who cannot live the way they want to live. Then why don't they? They don't know, and they don't even know they don't know. They lack understanding.

It's this terror barrier that makes people who want to buy something they want, back away, or when they go to move, but they don't. They want to change jobs, but they don't. They want to move to another city, but they don't. Why? Fear. Fear causes them to stay where they are. This is bondage. The comfort zone is like prison, except we hold the key.

When you get emotionally involved with an idea that is outside your comfort zone, different from your paradigm, or something you haven't done before, doubt, fear, and anxiety are triggered as you are about to act. This causes you to hit the terror barrier and bounce right back off it into bondage. You are so relieved to get back there. You're back where you feel comfortable.

You've cancelled the sale. You've decided not to move. You're going to stay in the job you don't like. At least you're comfortable. Then you start to reason and somehow justify your inaction. Now that's not a very good way to live.

This is something that everybody experiences if they're going to grow. Growth means you're going to hit that terror barrier. However, at least with understanding, you can continue to move forward, continue to act, even though you feel the fear. Abraham Maslow said, "When we are faced with change, we either step forward into growth, or we step back into safety."

So how do you break through the terror barrier to freedom? It takes one of two things: Either your goal needs to be something that you want so badly, it's worth failing for, or it takes just one, tiny additional ingredient; this one tiny, little thing will give you the courage to step through that terror barrier when you bump up against it. That one missing thing is *understanding*.

Even after you go through the terror barrier, the fear doesn't vanish straight away; you need to continue to act and go through the terror barrier many more times before you feel comfortable with the new way of doing things. Then ultimately, the new way becomes as comfortable as the old way once was, and this is now your new comfort zone.

Understanding leads to courage, and that's what you need to change your whole life. Courage. Courage to risk, and an expectation to win, with a measure of persistence.

> "The cave you fear to enter, holds the treasure you seek."
> Joseph Campbell

I love Joseph Campbell's words because they are so true. He says, "The cave you fear to enter, holds the treasure you seek."

****

Because the Silva Method changed my life so profoundly, I wrote to them to express my heartfelt gratitude. Without realising the power of my own words, in the subject line of the email, I wrote, "Australia Instructor DREAM."

See the original email below:

Fri, Oct 4, 2013, 11:47 PM

To: silvamethod@silvamethod.com

Attention Laura Silva - AUSTRALIA INSTRUCTOR DREAM

To the kind person receiving this mail,

Please can you pass this on to Laura Silva personally?

Thanking you in advance,

Jeanine

_____

Hi Laura

Firstly, may I say I'm honoured to be writing to you.

Brief Background:

I bought your Silva Manifesting program early 2012. I was really struggling in a new sales role in a multi-national company, and was "guided" to your website one evening searching for help, when I read a review of a person in my exact same situation that became top sales person in 6 months after practicing the Silva Method. Immediately I bought your programme online. (I'm a South African Italian, recently immigrated to Australia 3.5 years ago and the change of country and the job were both a massive challenge).

Cut a long story short: I "consumed" your Silva Manifesting program like a hungry animal, and needless to say, the same success happened to me too, in less than 6 months! I was top sales person in the Pacific Region and hold that position still to this day! In 2012 I smashed my sales target achieving 187%. This year, I made my annual target in August already, with some massive sales deals in the pipeline that should all close before end of Nov. I expect to achieve 200% of my target this year - or "better than that". I also won two awards at work. This amazing turnaround came from previously being in a very scary position of knowing if I don't turn things around and start achieving at work I will be asked to leave.

I have understood manifesting for several years already (since 2006) and have previously bought several other programmes too from authors such as Mike Dooley and Dr Wayne Dyer. I could honestly write a book on the series of amazing events over the past 7 years that have fallen in place like dominoes when I practice the techniques learned over the years. I actually had the privilege of meeting Mike Dooley when I attended his course in Sydney last year.

However, when I bought your program, Silva Manifesting, it was fresh, simple, well structured, practical, illuminating and most importantly, highly effective that always delivered results sooner than expected.

I am constantly learning, finding more information, raising the bar of my dreams, practicing meditations, visualisations and truly living deliberately, or as you say: living the life of my own design.

What next?

Why am I writing to you?

I have a burning desire to be a Silva Instructor. I live in Australia and see that there aren't any here.

My questions for you please:

What do I need to do to become a Silva Instructor in Australia?

Do I need to take the Silva Life Training Course and Silva Instructors Course?

If I fly to the USA to take the Silva Life Training Course and Silva Instructors Course, how long is it, (could they be soon after each other for practical purposes)?

Lastly, will you personally be delivering the program? (I would be honoured to meet you, and aspire to doing your Instructors Course led by you.

I so look forward to hearing back from you, and thank you sincerely for the wonderful work you do and for sharing the GREAT truths discovered by your amazing Blessed and God-inspired father.

With love and admiration

Jeanine Sciacca

Silva International wrote back, and I had a Skype conversation with the global training director, who informed me that I first needed to do the Silva training five times before qualifying for the instructor's course. So this was like a five- to ten-year plan for me, as it would mean travelling to the United States five times before becoming a trainer. The first opportunity I got to do the live training was in 2015. During that training, I had a meeting after hours one night, where it was explained to me that the journey to become a trainer would take at least five years.

A few months later, I got an email from Silva International saying that they believed in me and wanted me to become a trainer as soon as possible. They said if I could come to the United States (at short notice, like within a month), I could do the instructor's training, and they would certify me. Wow. I was blown away. This was a miracle. What an opportunity. What a blessing. I was so excited, but at the same time, I was feeling very unsure about the timing.

I was torn because I had just come back from a months' holiday in South Africa. I had not worked for four weeks, which in my world meant no income. Unexpectedly, this email arrived, offering me my dream on a silver platter, and it was four years earlier that the usual sequence of events to become a Silva Method trainer. My heart wanted to jump at it and make my dream come true, yet my head said, *Don't be crazy; you've just spent enough money already overseas and have not worked for four weeks. Come to your senses, woman. Reply and tell them you'll do it next year if the same offer is still on.*

I happened to be running a weekend retreat with another associate when this all happened, so during the vision board exercise, I mentioned to the entire group, quite casually, that I had a dilemma. All heads turned to me in surprise. *You* have a dilemma? Everyone was curious, as I was the one delivering the purpose, vision, and goals portion of the retreat that morning, so I guess they looked to me as the expert in the room, and here I was, admitting I had a dilemma. When I shared the story, the response I got was tremendous. Everyone told me there was no decision to be made; there was no dilemma. This was a no-brainer. They kept affirming, "This is your dream. What are you waiting for?"

To really prove the universe was guiding me, at this retreat, we had a psychic offering readings. This was something I had never done before; however, the opportunity was there, so I went for a reading. The dialogue went something like this:

Psychic: Did you lose a child?

Me: No.

Psychic: Do you have children?

Me: No.

Psychic: I'm picking up a young person here. Young enough to be your child.

Me: How old is this person?

Psychic: About twenty-one.

Me: Oh wow! Yes, I lost my younger brother when he was twenty-one. I was old enough to be his mother; I was forty-two when he passed on.

Psychic: He says you have potential travel coming up. He says you must go. Everything will work out. You must go. He says that you are struggling with the decision to go; however, he is really encouraging you to go—almost insisting.

When I got home from that retreat, I made peace with the decision to travel to the United States two weeks later. During my meditation that night, I went onto my knees and prayed, head down on the floor, "Father, I surrender. I trust your guidance. Please guide me. Thank you for this amazing opportunity. I have faith that You will look after me. You always have, and I know You always will. Thank you."

I surrendered and fully embraced this incredible miracle of an offer to become a Silva Method trainer at least four years earlier than expected.

The next day, I got a call from my accountant, who said, "Jeanine, I have good news. You'll be very happy with your tax return this year. There were some corrections made to the prior year that were owing to you, plus the NRAS [National Residential Affordability Scheme] properties have finally paid the money owing to you for the past two years."

The next day in the post, I received my tax return with a refund of over $41,000. God had truly blessed me

> "Faith is not belief without proof; it is trust without reservation."
> D. Elton Trueblood

and paved the way of my destiny. I dropped to my knees in gratitude and cried at the pathway opening before me, literally guiding my life. I could not stop praying the same prayer from John 11:41 over and over: "I thank Thee, Father, for Thou hast heard me. I thank Thee, Father, for Thou hast heard me."

I understood what it meant to *surrender*. When the door that's right for you opens, you have to have faith that all is according to some grand plan, some grand energy that guides your life; that is the same energy that guides this entire universe. This is why chapter 1 is about developing a constant connection to Source energy, from where all things come. James 1:17 says, "Every good and perfect gift that you receive comes from above." 1 Corinthians 8:6 says, "There is but one God, the Father, from whom all things come."

When I silenced my analytical, logical, and reasoning mind, which was filled with doubts about finances and forgoing my dream for short-term money matters, I stepped forward with faith, and Source energy took care of the rest, not just to get me by, but in a grand and deliberate way. In other words, saying, "Well done for following the path of your passion and purpose, trusting in my guidance. Here is everything you need and more to ensure you are supported, you are taken care of, you are loved, you are resourced, and you are given more than you need. So go forth, have fun, and make your dreams come true."

Through a sequence of miraculous events, this dream did come true, four years *earlier* than expected. When you're on the right path, the universe will conspire in your favour. You've just got to surrender and keep moving forward with trust and faith in a higher power that's guiding your life. In the words of D. Elton Trueblood, "Faith is not belief without proof; it is trust without reservation."

When there is passion, persistence, and the intention of adding value to others, the universe collaborates, and truly anything is possible. When doors open, keep moving in that direction. When doors close, it's a sign to change direction; have faith, and trust the process.

The notorious cherry on the cake for me was the amazing synchronicity when the date for my first Silva Method live training class was set. The original date had to be changed due to some circumstances, and the company promoting the event came back to me with November 26 as the final date. This was no other than Gianmarco's birthday. That was a blessing and a confirmation that my life was being guided. A sign for me that Giammi was my angel and somehow instrumental in the perfect unfolding of these events, from the time I was told by that psychic that my late brother was urging me to take that trip (against all of my logic), to receiving more money than I needed to assure me I was on track, to the date of my very first training day, when I stepping into my dream of being a Silva Method instructor: Giammi's birthday.

So today, I really am living my dream, and I'm not telling you this to boast or impress you. I'm telling you this because in the words of John Maxwell, "The two most important days of your life are the day you were born and the day you know *why* you were born." I can positively and confidently say that I know I was born to do this.

What Is Your Life Purpose?

In simple terms, your life purpose is your why. Ask yourself, Why do I exist? Why am I here? Why do I do what I do? What is my purpose?

Your life purpose is your compass. It is the filter through which you will make most of the decisions in your life.

When it comes to your life's purpose, there are a couple of things you should know:

- Your life's purpose is the mission you give yourself. It's not this obscure, mysterious thing that you've got to find, that is always eluding you. You choose your life purpose; however, it does need to fulfil certain criteria to be your true purpose and is not some self-indulgent ambitious undertaking.
- Your life purpose makes use of your talents, strengths, and gifts. There are certain things that you are good at, no matter what is going through your head when you read this. Many people say they don't have any special talents or gifts. This is just not true. They are just expressing a self-limiting belief or low self-esteem. Everyone has something they do better than most others. If you're unsure, think back over your life to what people have praised you for or what came easily to you, that you enjoyed doing because you do it effortlessly and you do it well. It could be something as simple as consoling a friend, cooking and baking, fixing things, being supportive to others in a time of need, being a good listener, taking care of a loved one who is sick, relating to children or animals, growing plants, whatever it may be. It does not have to be a specific talent like music or artistic expression, although these are definitely included too. The point is, it can be something we take for granted, yet it

makes a difference to people when we do it because we do it so well, and we do it with love.

- Your purpose is about serving others. If it does not involve others and is only about serving your own needs, it's not a life purpose. Your life purpose gives your life meaning, which in simple terms implies that it is meaningful to others. If you are living your life purpose, you are making a difference; you are solving or correcting problems to make this world a better place. You are adding value. Your life serves a beneficial and worthwhile purpose. Everything revolves around this central theme.

- Your purpose is something you are passionate about. It involves doing something that you absolutely love to do, that you would happily enjoy doing for free whenever you got the chance. It feels like fun, not like work, even though it could be deemed work. When you're doing it, your heart is in it, and you do it with love.

- It is something that when you get a glimpse of it, it calls you. It beckons you like a vocation. You feel drawn to it. It is as if this thing is just right for you.

- When you do this thing, people compliment you for it, perhaps even since you were a child. It's something that's an authentic expression of you that you do really well, almost effortlessly. It feels natural when you are doing it; however, there is always the potential to expand, grow, and master this craft, just like anything in life. You can always better your best, whether it be art, public speaking, business strategy, analytics, teaching, healing, music, design, sport, or coaching: the list goes on.

- It may be something that many people have a talent for; however, when *you* express this gift, it is unique. It is as unique as you are. It's difficult for anyone to copy you because your expression of this gift (even though that talent may be shared by many) is expressed through you unlike any other, and when you're doing it, you feel alive, you feel energised, you feel inspired, you feel like you're in your zone.

- Every time you take part in this activity or expression of yourself, you feel like you've had a wonderful day. If anyone asks you how your day was on a day that you were doing this activity, you would always answer that you had a brilliant day. It would leave you feeling fulfilled, uplifted, and purposeful, like it meant something. It leaves you feeling that you made a difference in somebody's life on that day. Deep inside, you know if you did more of that intentionally, with focus, time, and dedication, you would make an impact on people's lives.
- Your life's purpose is like your sun, to use the analogy of the solar system. All planets revolve around the sun. In the same way, all your choices and activities revolve around this central purpose. This makes it easier to make decisions. It becomes your filter through which you become more discerning. For example, let's say you were invited to a social function that you'd love to attend for the fun of it, yet on the same date, you had the opportunity to do this activity that would add value to others and which you absolutely love doing. Making the decision would be easy for you. You would do the one that leaves you fulfilled and feeling purposeful.

Ways to Find Your Life's Purpose

I remember the words of my mentor: "In your passion lies your God-given purpose." Pay close attention to anything you are passionate about. *Anything.* From dancing to painting your friends' nails, from helping vulnerable children to building things out of wood or planning amazing holidays. Anything.

There was a young man who loved watching movies. That was his passion. He watched every movie that came out as soon as it was released. He would always be the one telling his friends if they should watch it or not. This man was Roger Ebert. He became the best film critic in America. He won the Pulitzer Prize for criticism in 1975, and in 2005, he became the first film critic to receive a star on the Hollywood Walk of Fame. When we are passionate about something, we have the fire inside to create great things.

To get an idea of what you are passionate about, ask yourself these questions whilst in a calm and relaxed state:

- What do you love so much, you'd do it for nothing, yet you'd do it so well people want to pay you for it?
- What's close to your heart? What do you like reading about or watching or researching online? It could be anything from conservation of this planet to great food recipes. Many people have passions they aren't even aware of.
- What makes you forget about the world around you? Time flies when you're having fun, they say. What is it that you are doing when time flies and you're having fun?
- What did you love doing as a child? What did you love doing as a teenager? What childhood dreams did you have about yourself and your life?
- What do people praise and compliment you for?
- What do friends, colleagues, and family turn to you for? How do you help them? Think about the times your friends have come to you for help or advice. This shows the areas in which your friends class you as a valuable source of knowledge; it could be something you didn't even realise you were good at.
- What do you love to discuss with your closest friends? Generally, we talk to those we trust about things that mean a lot to us. This is often a great indicator of your life purpose.
- If all work paid the same, what would you be doing?
- If you had all the money you ever needed, how would you spend your time?
- What do you dream about? Many people have dreams but choose not to pursue them due to the financial risks or fear

of failure. Start thinking about your dream in a more positive light, saying to yourself, "It's possible." It may not be probable for you at this stage; however, it is possible. The Bible says, "With God, all things are possible." This is *all* things, no exclusions. You cannot have a dream without also having the potential to fulfil it. Therefore, instead of telling yourself it's too difficult or you won't succeed, hold that image in your mind. See yourself doing it in your mind, visualise yourself doing it, and keep telling yourself, "It's possible." Over time, you'll convince yourself that it *is* possible, and whatever you believe, you achieve. If it's something you are passionate about that can serve others or make this world a better place, you'll get the limitless energy, enthusiasm, and courage to take steps in that direction. Consider that it could truly be your life's purpose. Make a concerted effort to suspend negative thoughts that could hold you back from achieving your life purpose.

If you are unsure, don't feel disheartened; it can take a while to fathom what you are passionate about, so spend your time doing more of what you find enjoyable. Try new things. Experiment with any idea that you think will be fun and that excites you. I tried so many things and did many courses, looking for a hobby that really sticks. I love photography, as an example. I invested in good cameras and have taken thousands of photographs, and in that time, I had a lot of fun, yet I also realised I wouldn't want to do this full time. It was more a hobby. I've taken up musical instruments like the piano, flute, and drums and went for lessons. In my job, I changed career several times. You have to experiment in life and have many experiences that can help shape your likes and dislikes. Give yourself the time and the opportunities to find that thing that you are truly passionate about. Eventually, you will discover your life purpose. What it takes is three things:

1. A true desire to discover your life purpose, with the intention of serving others with it.
2. A constant question in your heart (not head) about what you really love to spend your time doing.
3. An open mind that it is possible to live your purpose every day, even if right now, you think it's improbable. It is *possible*.

CHAPTER 3

Developing Your Intuition

Wayne Dyer said, "If prayer is us talking to God, then intuition is God talking to us." I love that. This has to be the best way of putting it. Intuition is a sense that we all possess, just like sight, hearing, or taste, whether we use it or not, whether we trust it or not, whether we are even aware of it or not.

You came into this world with this inner guidance system that is termed your intuition. Imagine you are a vehicle going around this world in your human body, and you want to find your treasure, which is your happiness, your purpose, so that you can live your best life, fulfilled and content. Now imagine that your GPS to getting you there is Source energy, from where all things come. Source energy is your perfect GPS because Source is omnipotent (all powerful), omniscient (all knowing), and omnipresent (ever-present) and knows what is best for you. Your intuition is the signal of this GPS. It is the communication between your vehicle's guidance system and the satellite, which is the Source of all knowing.

When looking at it that way, refining and developing your intuition has got to be your highest priority, alongside developing a constant connection to Source energy and finding your life's purpose. In fact, you are *guided* to finding your life's purpose when you listen to your intuition.

Looking back on my own life, the intuitive steps that led me to finding my treasure were what Dyer calls quantum moments. They are vivid, surprising, benevolent, and enduring: vivid in that they are intense enough for us to notice every detail and to remember them forever. They are surprising: unexpected, uninvited, and unforeseen. Quantum moments are also benevolent; in other words, they come with the feelings of peace, serenity, and bliss. The fourth quality of a quantum moment is that it never goes away. That moment is burned into our consciousness, in a vivid picture that won't be forgotten. I've heard it described as being a warm shower running inside of you whose gracious imprint endures into infinity. You never forget that moment.

One intuitive step in my life was the day I watched the *Minute with Maxwell* daily inspiration video that hit my inbox, and at the end of the video was a button on the webpage that read "Join the John Maxwell Team." The day I clicked on that button, I got goose bumps all over, because I knew this was going to change my destiny. I clicked on it and remember that *knowing* feeling, that intuitive hunch that this is the thing that will take me closer to where all of me was yearning to go, even though I had no idea what that was or what it looked like.

Another intuitive quantum moment was the day I delivered my very first leadership talk; my colleague asked me how I enjoyed delivering it, and I heard myself say, "I loved it! I loved it with a passion."

I had spiritual chills pouring all over me, from the top of my head all the way down my body, because in that nanosecond, I realised I had just declared my passion, wherein I knew my God-given purpose lay, adding value to others and helping them become the grandest version of themselves to make a positive impact in this world.

After a year of knowing my purpose was to be a speaker, trainer, and coach and finding myself still stuck in a corporate job, desperate to find that golden bridge out of the corporate world to live my dream, I strategised and planned what this financial bridge could look like. It came through investment property. I love property and have always been a keen investor. I did a course during that year on renovating and flipping properties, and I worked out that if I flipped four houses a year, I could earn the same money as in my corporate job. I woke up one day and had this flash of intuitive insight: *Call Mike* (he sells investment property, and I had bought two from him a couple of years prior) *and ask him if he would like to be a third partner in a company that renovates and flips houses.* The other partner would be my friend Pearly, an architect who did the renovating course with me. When I picked up the phone to call Mike, I had that quantum experience. I believed that I had an offer he couldn't refuse, as he would reap a good share of the profits for little work, as I only wanted his expertise on what suburbs to focus on, no other work at all.

When I called that day, he listened and then replied, "Forget about renovating; that's too much work. Come and join me in selling new investment properties. I've known you for a while; you're great at sales. You love property, and you'll be great at it."

After that phone call, which was in a small private boardroom at work, I sat down, dropped my head between my knees, and thanked God over and over, as tears rolled down my cheeks, for giving me more than I could ask for. I was overwhelmed with gratitude. Why? Well, two years prior, when I met Mike for the very first time, he gave me a tour of the Central Coast area north of Sydney, showing me all the infrastructure changes and the reasons for growth of the investment property I decided to buy from him.

When we said goodbye, standing in the carpark of a shopping centre where my car was parked, I remember thinking, *I would do anything to do what you do. It would be a dream job working with you. I love property, I love sales, and I love what you do for a life, not a living.*

I also made a point of giving him my business card to make sure he knew I was in a consultative selling role, hoping that maybe, just maybe, one day he may be looking for a passionate, crazy little Italian from South Africa, who loves property and sales, and perhaps may just cast a glance my way; who knows?

Here I was, two years later, looking to find my golden bridge out of the corporate world to be financially secure, whilst ensuring I still had lots of free time, so that I could build my speaking, training and coaching business, which is my passion and purpose, and Mike asks me to join him as an independent consultant, working for myself. Wow. I would make good money and have enough free time to build my business. I immediately said yes. A few weeks later, I signed an agreement with Mike and asked him if I could refer clients right away, as I had people in mind who would be keen to buy.

He said, "Sure, I'll even pay you a commission for the deals I do on your behalf, until you leave your corporate job. Consider it your training. Whilst you give your company notice, we can do the appointments after hours, so there's no interfering with your day job."

If I sold one property a month, it would be enough to cover my expenses. During my notice period, I sold four in the first month.

When you're on the right track in life, the universe paves the way forward. This was a sign to keep moving in this direction. Again, the universe was saying, "Well done for following the path of your passion and purpose, trusting in my guidance; here is everything you need and more, to ensure you are supported, you are taken care of, you are loved, you are resourced, and you are given more than you need. So go forth, have fun, and make your dreams come true."

In the book *The Alchemist* by Paulo Coelho, the old king says, "It's called the principle of favourability, beginner's luck. Because life wants you to achieve your Personal Legend."

When it comes to your intuition, there are a couple of things you should know:

- Intuition requires a relaxed state. When you are stressed, it is like static in your GPS signal. Your connection is literally breaking up. You need to learn the art and skill of remaining calm at all times (or as often as possible). Learning to destress is a skill to develop, like going to the gym to get fit. Once you know how to recognise stress and dissolve it quickly, it will allow you to return to your centred, balanced, relaxed self, and you will have more access to your intuition.
- Your intuition is as unique as you are. For some, it may be a little voice in your head or in one ear, sometimes the left, sometimes the right. For others, it is a flash of insight or an image that pops into your head. For others, it can be a gut feeling or having those spiritual chills come over you when you think a thought or when you need to be aware of a certain truth; it's confirmation you're on the right track.
- Your intuition will always guide you in the right direction. Your intuition is a pure, sacred guidance system that, when you're tuned in, will literally guide your life to the quickest, happiest, most fulfilling, and most loving experiences for you, where all abundance and success will manifest around you, as you become aligned with who you truly are and express your authentic self fully.
- Intuition is fast, is quick, and doesn't hang around. It comes in a flash. If it's an idea, write it down immediately because you may not remember it.
- Einstein said, "The intellect has little to do on the road to discovery. There comes a leap in consciousness, call it intuition or what you will, and the solution comes to you,

and you don't know how or why." Intuition is often the wisest solution that you *know* is right without rhyme, reason, or explanation.

- Intuition's polar opposite is logic. So for all those left-brained analytical people, be prepared for it to take more time to refine. Be patient with yourself. You will get better with practice. If you get a hunch and then analyse it, you're probably going off on the wrong track. The minute you engage the logical brain, that is not intuition.
- Logic is the opposite of intuition.

Ways to Develop Your Intuition

- First and foremost, learn how to remain calm, relaxed, and focused, no matter what is happening around you. The best way to do this is to meditate daily. The end.
- Create a discipline of daily meditation. If you don't know how, download the Silva Method Long Relaxation Meditation from my website, www.silvamethodaustralia.com.au. If you practice it daily, you will condition your mind and your body to recognise the feeling of being relaxed. Over time, with daily practice, you'll *become* that person who is always calm. This will give you maximum access to your intuition.
- Awareness is key to becoming conscious of that gut feeling, or that hunch, or spiritual chills (goose bumps), or that little voice, or that flash of insight, or that vision, or that dream. First awareness, then take action. The more aware you are of your intuition and follow its guidance, almost as a personal project, the more you'll come to know and trust that feeling.
- Notice how many good ideas or intuitive insights you get when you're daydreaming, or having a shower, or walking, or listening to relaxing music. Why? You are relaxed. Your logical, analytical mind is not active. This is a point of reference for you, so note it.

- Whenever you have to make an important decision, take time out, relax somewhere undisturbed, and ask yourself if A or B is right for you, then pay attention to whatever happens. Don't overthink it. Remain relaxed. You may get a feeling or a flash of insight or an idea that guides you. Trust this, and move with this guidance, not your head or cognitive thoughts.
- Always trust your intuition. Always. If it ever lets you down, go back and work out why. Was it fear? Was it wishful thinking? Was it a projection of your own agenda or conditioning onto a situation? This will help you refine it and learn to know what true intuitive insight is and is not.
- Develop many points of reference. The more points of reference you have, the more you can become discerning about how you sense intuition. The best way to refine and develop your intuitive abilities is with more and more points of reference.
- In the Silva Method, which is a four-day dynamic meditation programme, two full days are dedicated to developing intuition. We play fun games and get immediate feedback to develop many points of reference. It is as important to get accurate hits as it is to get inaccurate hits. This way, we get to distinguish between how we sensed it when we were correct and when we were off the mark. The results people get in just a few days of attending the course blows their socks off. They realise just how intuitive we all really are and how much we can actually develop when we have a trusted and proven method.
- You could also play games at home with a partner using playing cards, and intentionally tune in, while remaining very relaxed, to sense whether the card is red or black, or the suit or the number, or all of the above. Five out of twenty correct hits is average and probably a lucky guess. So with practice, if your score goes up, you know you're tuning in better.

- Wherever you go, try to sense the answer, or what will happen, or how much it costs, or what the time is, or the score, or the weight, or even stand on the platform where you sense the train door will stop and notice, when you're aware and intentionally tuning in, how much better your intuitive sensing is.

- Have fun with strangers or people you don't know too much about, and before they tell you anything about themselves, ask them if you can guess their hobbies, car, pets, children, birth month, or food tastes. Have a desire to tune in and go with whatever pops in your head; with their feedback, you can make points of reference as to how you sensed it when you were accurate and inaccurate.

- Practice makes improvement. Intuition is a skill, and like any skill, it can be improved with deliberate practice.

- Whenever you know what a person was about to say, tell them. They are probably on your wavelength. That just means you're tuned in, like the frequency of a radio station. There are hundreds of radio, television, Wi-Fi, and Bluetooth signals at any given place at any time, but you only hear the ones you tune into. This is the same as intuition. So when you feel you're tuned it, make it fun and see how much you can detect from that person. Play guessing games: what number am I thinking of? What colour? What fruit? What car? Pay attention to how you sensed it when you were correct versus when you were incorrect. Both are important. Don't let your ego ever get in the way. It is not a test; it helps you learn about yourself and improve, so be open to not being perfect.

Refine and develop your intuition, which is the most valuable sense you can have, because it will lead you to your treasure. In *The Alchemist*, intuition is referred to as the omens. It is so eloquently described in these words of this beautiful fable, which contains some noteworthy truths:

In order to find the treasure, you will have to follow the omens. God has prepared a path for everyone to follow. You just have to read the omens that he left for you.

"Learn to recognize omens, and follow them," the old king had said....

The boy thought about his treasure. The closer he got to the realization of his dream, the more difficult things became. It seemed as if what the old king had called "beginner's luck" were no longer functioning. In his pursuit of the dream, he was being constantly subjected to tests of his persistence and courage. So he could not be hasty, nor impatient. If he pushed forward impulsively, he would fail to see the signs and omens left by God along his path.

Then, ... the omens will abandon you, because you've stopped listening to them.... You'll spend the rest of your days knowing that you didn't pursue your Personal Legend, and that now it's too late.

CHAPTER 4

Living on Purpose

Finding your purpose is so important, as it provides that filter through which you make all your decisions that take you towards your vision for your life. This then guides your next steps, which are your goals.

You could say the vision represents *what* you are doing with your life, the goal represents the various aspects of *how* you're doing it, and your purpose explains *why*. It is very important that your purpose, vision, and goals are in harmony.

You need three tools to live on purpose, create your vision, and achieve your goals:

1. Understanding
2. Awareness
3. Self-evaluation

Understanding

If you just think of the term "living on purpose," it's all about intention. It means you are intentional and deliberate about your life. You are thinking, planning, and acting on purpose. Living on purpose has a lot of power behind it, because it's for a purpose greater than yourself. It is for a grander purpose than just satisfying your personal ambitions. Living on purpose means you have an intention to serve others. This intention to serve is what gives you the motivation and inclination to develop and use more of your potential; it requires you to go beyond just your needs. This is why you were born. Yes, you were born for a specific purpose, and this purpose is backed by an intention to serve. All great leaders, throughout history, had a grand purpose which benefitted many others, and this grand purpose caused them to rise to the occasion and become the grandest versions of themselves.

You have the potential to do far greater things than you could ever begin to imagine and make an impact in your home, in your job, in your community, and in the world at large. Your potential is unlimited. *Unlimited.* For you to unlock more of your potential and grow to become the grandest version of yourself, you need to have a vision for your life. Proverbs 29:18 says, "Without a vision the people perish." This means that people live lost, lost without a purpose, vision, or goals.

Awareness

Creating a vision for your life is a very powerful and creative process, whether you're aware of it or not. Therefore, all personal development gurus and coaches encourage you to write down your visions and goals. The truth is that you are creating your reality every second, whether you're aware of it or not. This is a universal law, the law of attraction or the law of vibration, and it does not require your belief in it to work in your life. The sooner you take 100 percent responsibility for your life, knowing that you *do* co-create your own reality, with your thoughts and feelings, the better. It is the understanding and awareness that helps you guide this natural process of creation that is taking place in your life, either unconsciously or consciously.

When you create a vision statement, it starts to mould the energy that creates your reality because the thoughts about your vision cause you to feel emotions (automatically). The emotions you feel change your vibration; everything you experience as your reality is always a vibrational match to what you are putting out there. Writing it out is a very important step because it clarifies the vision and gives it order.

It is the vision in your mind, harmonising with your purpose, which creates the inspiration that causes you to stretch yourself. You need to stretch to become a grander version of yourself and realise your potential. The vision you hold also determines the frequency of your thoughts. The larger and clearer the vision, the bigger, better, and more effective the ideas will be that flow into your consciousness. It is important to note that ideas are the first manifestation. When you have a vision for your life, driven by purpose, and you get an idea, often at the most random of moments, that is the first manifestation. All ideas are spiritual seeds. Just like seeds, ideas have the potential to become magnificent creations *if* they are put into the right environment conducive to their growth. Become very aware of ideas; always note them down and follow up with intentional action. This is how you literally co-create your own reality.

The writing of your vision should be fun and exciting, and a feeling of hopeful expectation should fill your soul. Your vision statement will ultimately be the highest expression of your awareness at that time for your life and for your purpose.

From your vision statement, you will then begin to identify your short-term and long-term goals. Your goals will come from your vision, sometimes directly from your vision, and sometimes as a way for you to live your vision. The biggest challenge in creating the vision is your own inner voice's need to know how you are going to fulfil them. This is going to be your big test. If there is one golden rule for the creative and manifesting process, it is this: Suspend the need to know how. This is an essential principle for manifesting what you want. Don't ask how. Don't think about how. Just stay focused on your vision and get emotionally involved with the idea of living it. Let it excite you. Fall in love with your vision. Get emotionally engaged.

The reason you must avoid thinking *how,* is that it engages the analytical, thinking, and reasoning mind. A very real part of a reasoning mind is the need to know how, and it gets stuck if it's not satisfied with an answer. Doubt will creep in, followed by fear and indecision. I'm sure you've heard the saying that doubt kills more dreams than failure ever will. This is very true. The mind begins the rejection of the idea process and begins to reason why you can't. It accesses all your past results, your old files, and begins to run those programmes through your awareness. If you have not done what you envision for yourself, then it reasons that you cannot do it in the future, either, because you've never done it before.

This is why visualising is so important when it comes to manifesting your vision and dreams. When visualising, you see yourself doing, being, and having whatever it is in the mind's eye. The subconscious mind cannot distinguish between imagination and reality. This is the single most important fact you'll ever need to know to co-create the life of your dreams. In the words of Napoleon Hill: "What the mind can conceive and believe, it can achieve." Therefore, if the mind sees you repeatedly achieving your vision and goals, even though it is in your imagination, it will believe that you are achieving it, and whatever you believe becomes your reality.

In the initial stages of moving towards your grand vision, stay in the land of possibility to prevent the mind from rejecting the vision or idea. I have used this for years to keep me positive, motivated, and focused on my vision, and I keep affirming to myself that it's possible. Whenever your relentless mind tries to figure out how you will succeed, instead, affirm to yourself, *it's possible,* and ensure that you visualise the achievement of the goals and vision, with the coherent emotions of already having accomplished it. The emotions are the creative force. The emotions are the signal you emit to the universe; many refer to this as your vibration, and your reality is always a vibrational match to what you are feeling. These emotions attract the events, people, and circumstances into your life in order to achieve your goals, because your reality will always match that frequency. Trust that Source energy will take care of the details and know that the how is not your responsibility to figure out.

Your job is to create a grand vision for your life, which is rewarding, inspiring, and significant. Remember to dream big. Remember that the sky isn't the limit; your vision is. It was Norman Vincent Peale who said, "Shoot for the moon. Even if you miss, you'll land among the stars." If you're aiming for something, even if you don't achieve it, you'll still be somewhere better than where you started. "Most people fail in life not because they aim too high and miss. Most people fail in life because they aim too low and hit," Michelangelo once said.

> "Shoot for the moon. Even if you miss, you'll land among the stars."
> Norman Vincent Peale

Once you've set your intention with your vision statement, detach from the outcome. Being attached to the outcome only hampers the creative process. Trust and have faith that the how will be taken care of, and go with the flow. If the outcome is not exactly what you expected, it is probably because something better is coming, so stay open to a higher power guiding the process and your life.

> "Most people fail in life not because they aim too high and miss. Most people fail in life because they aim too low and hit." Michelangelo

When it comes to your goals, they are the stepping stones towards your vision. These may be short term or long term. Goals are an important part of the creative process, of creating the life that you want. The purpose of goals is to benchmark your progress; they help you grow into the person who is living your purpose and vision.

It's often said that goals need to excite and scare you at the same time. They will excite you because it must be something you want, and you must really want it. They will scare you because it is not in harmony with your old conditioning (paradigm). Your goals come from a totally different dimension of thought. When the new goal and the old conditioning come together, it creates the emotion of fear. This is an automatic response for all of us and will never change. Therefore, to have the understanding and the awareness of how you are wired is so important for you to be able to move forward, *with* the fear. This fear is precisely what keeps you stuck in your tracks, producing the same results, year after year. Any thought or idea that is different from what you have done in the past (and will most likely be different from your subconscious mind's conditioning) will cause doubt and fear, which is expressed through your body as anxiety. Any idea in harmony with your current paradigm or current results is comfortable; that's why it's termed the comfort zone. Even if the current conditions are making you unhappy and the latest ideas or goals will make you happier, if the idea is outside of our comfort zone, it will produce fear; the only thing that varies is the degree. Just do what you can, with what you've got, from where you are. Sometimes, when the whole vision is far out of your comfort zone, the best plan is based on one single step. Just take the next step.

To succeed, you must face the thing you fear. Moving forward in the face of fear and remaining emotionally involved with the higher ideal is the process that alters old conditioning. Abraham Maslow said, "You will either step forward into growth or back into safety."

> "Fear, the worst of all enemies can be effectively cured by forced repetition of acts of courage."
> Napoleon Hill

You will ultimately realise that when you face the thing you fear, the fear leaves you. This is freedom. Your freedom lies on the other side of fear. Napoleon Hill said, "Fear, the worst of all enemies can be effectively cured by forced repetition of acts of courage."

Self-Evaluation

Now that we've covered the areas of *understanding* and *awareness* about living on purpose, let's explore *self-evaluation*. Self-evaluation is a powerful tool for personal growth and for becoming a deliberate creator of your life experience. Every experience, good or bad, is feedback. Every experience is a manifestation of what's been going on inside you most recently. The more aware you become of this feedback and evaluate each situation by asking, "How did I create this?" the more you refine your ability to co-create your own reality. Your experience is your guide to keep you on track.

When you create what you don't want, it helps you refine what you do want, and this makes you more intentional about co-creating better circumstances. It also teaches you about yourself, so you can get to know your personal code of success. Not getting what you want can be a result of not visualising daily, not visualising with emotion, or having worrying or contradictory opinions, negative thoughts, or self-doubt. Resistance to a situation or person also puts you into a negative state that interferes with your ability to manifest what you want. Every experience is a learning event, if you reflect on the experience and evaluate it. Self-evaluation produces valuable insights for you to develop and polish your natural creative process.

When it comes to living on purpose, here are a couple of things you should know:

- Acknowledge that you are a powerful and natural creator of your life's circumstances and events. Whether you're aware of it or not, you do create your own reality. Your job is to become more aware and direct this natural process.

- Realise that your self-value is not determined by your results. You are not your results. Your results are feedback as to how well you are consciously directing your energy to intentionally live on purpose and co-create the life you want.
- Write a vision statement for yourself. Here are a few guidelines:
  - o Write it in the present tense.
  - o Write all statements in positive terms.
  - o Start the vision statement with: I'm so happy and grateful now that ...
  - o Keep it in very general terms; the more general the better. This allows the universe to deliver what is most beneficial for you, which may be better than your specific ideas.
  - o Cover all areas of your life: career, health, relationships, finances, fun and recreation, spirituality, and community.
  - o Your vision needs to be rewarding, not realistic. Dream big.
- Write short- and long-term goals in specific and measurable terms that are aligned with your vision and in complete harmony with your purpose. Your goals will be stepping stones in the materialisation of your entire vision.
- Write down the benefits of achieving these goals. How will your life be different and better, and how will this positively benefit others?
- Add time lines to your goals.
- Suspend the need to know how.
- Visualise daily, for as little as five minutes or better, and get emotionally engaged.
  - o It is essential that you can visualise yourself already in possession of the goal and feel how it feels to

have accomplished it. Your emotions are the creative force.

- Detach from the outcome and have faith that Source energy will support you, then surrender and go with the flow.

CHAPTER 5

Living a Guided Life

When you have discovered your life's purpose and live each day trusting your intuition, you begin to live what I call a guided life. Living a guided life is the most gratifying, rewarding, and joyous experience. The result of this awareness is that your life is guided by some omnipotent power that fills this entire universe with perfection and love. It is more than a seeking of this guidance; it is a dependence on this guidance. Dependence is trust, reliance, and confidence that firstly, this power is never going to lead you in the wrong direction, and secondly, it will give you the guidance and all the resources you are seeking. Period. Matthew 7:7 says, "Ask and it will be given to you; seek and you will find."

Learning to live a guided life takes time. It is a process of learning to trust this guidance. It initially guides you with what I refer to as God's silent, gentle, and perfect guidance. With experience and developing more faith, you then seek this guidance out proactively by asking for it, expecting it, looking for signs that indicate it, trusting it, surrendering to it, and serving it with your whole heart in full faith, and that's when the true miracles happen. Let me give you some examples.

In the year before I left my corporate job, conditions and circumstance seemed to heat up around me, almost as though it was pushing me out. (Remember that I had this inkling that my life purpose was to be a speaker, trainer, and coach of leadership. I just didn't know how it would manifest and what it would look like.) My most valued team members were made redundant, and most were not replaced, leaving the extra workload on my shoulders. The workload increased, and the support decreased. As the experience got more and more unbearable, my desire for a change grew stronger, and I became more creative with finding solutions for myself to get me out of the corporate world.

Initially, I started looking for other corporate jobs, and the day I got the chance to apply for a job at Google, I thought I hit the jackpot. This was going to be my big break. I did everything I could to land this job, from visualising daily, to using affirmations, to working tirelessly to get my resume as best as I could, as well as the cover letter. I even asked the few contacts I had at Google to help put in a good word for me. When nothing materialised, not even a face-to-face interview, I was so disappointed. I wanted a change so badly.

At the same time my intuition was trying to tell me it was not the right path. If I got the job at Google, it would take me at least nine months to become highly effective and competent in the new role, then at least two years to prove myself as being consistently good. All this energy invested in the corporate agenda would just delay me from living my purposeful life and stepping into my freedom. I was looking for a quick fix to make things right, and not the right thing. The closed door was God guiding me. My earnest desire was to live my purpose and working for Google was not it. At the time, I could not see that it was as a blessing in disguise, moving me towards something better and sooner.

When I got over not getting the job at Google, I was still seeking my way out of the corporate world, eager to live my dream of speaking, training and coaching, as I already had my John Maxwell certification. I got this amazing idea. Remember: An idea is a spiritual seed, so I acted upon it straight away. I contacted Peter, who I met a few weeks prior. Peter had his own training business for over twenty years and was relatively successful. However, he had hit his own glass ceiling as to how much more he could do to grow his business. Peter did an internet search, looking for a John Maxwell-certified trainer and coach. As the universe would coordinate all things, he reached out to me and asked me to share my experience of joining the John Maxwell Team with him. He wanted to see if it would be of value to him and his business. I did this and eagerly spent about three hours with him in a coffee shop, sharing all my knowledge and insights, not only about the JMT, but also how he could grow his business with the tools I had learned along the way. He was very encouraged at the time and got a lot of worthwhile information out of the meeting; he told me he learnt a lot and what I suggested was refreshing, innovating, and valuable.

So the idea I got a few weeks later was to contact Peter and make him an offer he couldn't refuse. I proposed to be an extension of his business that would not cost him a cent, by offering John Maxwell leadership courses and Mastermind classes to his client base. These courses and Masterminds would be on subjects, themes, and topics that he was not offering (with him referring me, of course) and share the proceeds with Peter. This way, he could offer more breadth in his business to what he was already doing, increasing his billing hours, which would increase his income, and it would not cost him a dollar to have me work *for* him, independently. He would also get the benefit of the JMT content that could be offered to his clients without him having to incur the cost of joining the JMT and studying all the content and preparing it. I had already done all that preparation and was ready to hit the ground running.

I, on the other hand, would benefit from having immediate access to an established client base that already trusted and liked him. As I developed my own client base, independent of Peter, I was happy to offer them all the courses he did, and I would introduce Peter to my clients so he could expand his client base that way, as well. Well, when I presented him with my proposal, which I was convinced he would not refuse, guess what? He did refuse. Again, I was so disappointed. I even went as far as emailing my presentation proposal to another JMT member I trusted, asking for his feedback to see where I had gone wrong. He said he would jump at it; it was a win-win situation. Peter had nothing to lose and everything to gain. At the time, I was left disappointed and confused as to what more I could have done. In hindsight, again, God was guiding me in a better direction. Closed doors are a sign that better things are ahead; have faith.

I offered a similar proposal to a woman who had her own business working for herself. I got similar feedback, that what I could bring to the table was very valuable, yet it never materialised. This door also closed, and several others, when I approached established training companies. All these experiences that I thought were things not working out for me were actually part of a bigger picture that *was*, in fact, working out for me better than expected. This is what I term God's silent, gentle, and perfect guidance.

In the months that followed, I expressed deep gratitude to God for all these gentle nudges, leading me in a specific direction, because I realised that God had the faith in me that I never had in myself. How do I know

> "Sometimes we need to borrow someone else's belief in us, before our own belief kicks in."
>
> Les Brown

this? A few months later, when I was offered that paid speaking gig on leadership at a corporate convention, I realised that this was guidance too. This guidance was letting me know that I could trust myself and stand confidently in my knowledge, my speaking skills, and my ability to deliver value, and the proof was the money they were willing to pay me for it. I did not *need* another person or business on which to hitch my wagon of dreams. I could do this on my own, and so I should. Another sign was when Silva International offered me the opportunity to become a certified Silva Method trainer four years earlier than expected. This was guidance too. God again nudged me forward, opening doors to lead me towards my higher purpose and passion, creating conditions for me to believe in myself more. Silva International believed in me. That corporate sponsor paying me for that leadership speaking gig believed in me. Les Brown says, "Sometimes we need to borrow someone else's belief in us, before our own belief kicks in."

Signs will always show up to guide you if you are open to them, believe in them, and expect them. During my first Silva Method live training class, Marie, one of my friends, who was a student in the class, came up to me in the tea pause during the intuition part of the training. She had a look on her face that told me I needed to stop whatever I was doing and listen to her.

She had tears in her eyes from emotion overflowing and said to me, "I know this may sound crazy, but I just need to say it. This doesn't come from me; I just need to say it. Your angel brother Giammi is in the room with us. He has been here all day. There are twelve chairs that we keep moving around during group work, and we are only eleven students. As I'm telling you this, I have goose bumps all over."

Listening to Marie, I got goose bumps too, or what I like to refer to as spiritual chills, from head to toe, and tears rolled down my cheeks, because I knew in my heart that this was a clear message from Giammi. He was around and aware of me. Along my journey, it was Giammi who inspired me to never give up on my dream of becoming a Silva trainer, so this message meant so much to me. I was overcome with gratitude and emotion. Since that day, every time I train the Silva Method, I get some clear sign that Giammi is around, whether it be a feather, a bird following me, a song on the radio that reminds me of him, or a message via one of my students, like the message from Marie.

One night, whilst setting up for my Silva Method class the following day, I had an amazing conversation with a staff member at the venue about the fact that plants have a consciousness. This is something few people are aware of, yet it was scientifically proven over 150 years ago in India and then by Cleve Backster in the 1960s. This young man knew about this and was telling me about his grandmother, who loved plants and had so many of them, and when she passed on, all her plants died, even though other people were taking care of them.

I shared other extraordinary stories with him, such as the story of a man in South Africa known as the elephant whisperer. Soon after he passed on, two herds of wild South African elephants arrived at the house of the late author Lawrence Anthony, the conservationist who saved their lives. These elephants had made their way through the Zululand bush, traveling for twelve hours, until they reached his house.

The formerly violent rogue elephants, destined to be shot a few years ago as pests, were rescued and rehabilitated by Anthony, who had grown up in the bush and became known as the elephant whisperer. For two days, the herds loitered at Anthony's rural compound on the vast Thula Thula game reserve in the South African KwaZulu, saying goodbye to the man they loved. But how did they know he had died?

There were two elephant herds at Thula Thula. According to Anthony's son Dylan, both arrived at the family compound shortly after his death. "They had not visited the house for a year and a half, and it must have taken those elephants about twelve hours to make the journey," Dylan is quoted in various local news accounts. "The first herd arrived on Sunday and the second herd, a day later. They all hung around for about two days before making their way back into the bush."

If plants can sense death (which Backster proved in his experiment with a polygraph machine hooked up to a plant; that reacted after some brine shrimp died), then certainly elephants can sense the death of someone they loved. As we spoke, this young staff member reminded me so much of my late brother Giammi and was about the same age as Giammi before he passed on, at the age of twenty-one.

After I shared such stories and described what we teach in Silva Intuition training, this young man inspired me by telling me that the work I was doing was a blessing to people; he asked me how I got into it. I ended up sharing my story about Giammi and explained how he inspired me to follow my dream, especially since his passing. Getting in the car that night to go home, I switched on the radio, and a song I dedicated to Giammi many years before immediately came on. When I heard it, I knew Giammi was around. It was Savage Garden's song, "I Knew I Loved You before I Met You," except this time, I heard the words properly for what seemed like the first time:

> Maybe it's intuition,

> But some things you just don't question,

> Like in your eyes, I see my future in an instant.

For me, the meaning of those words, on that particular night, were very different. I was setting up for intuition training, and the first line of the song says, "Maybe it's intuition." That is no coincidence. As I heard these words, I knew Giammi was with

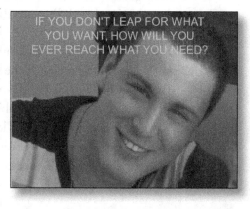

me. And when I heard the line that says, "Like in your eyes I see my future in an instant," I burst into tears because the photo I always keep on my vision board of Giammi's face, which has the quote that gave me the courage to follow my dreams, was like looking into Giammi's eyes every day when I looked at my vision board. This gave me the hope and determination to believe in my dreams and create my future of becoming a Silva Method trainer.

Those words seemed different that night and perfect for that moment in time: In your eyes, I see my future in an instant, now perfect. I cried out of love, gratitude, and emotion as the song played. It was the song I dedicated to Giammi; there was no mistaking that this was a sign, a message, and a spiritual connection in that moment. It's a feeling, it's overwhelming, and you know it's real. For me, it was a confirmation that I was on the right path, that somehow Giammi and other higher forces were guiding my life and celebrating the journey I was on. I was in alignment with my purpose, with God, and with my higher self (or what we may term our soul).

When it comes to living a guided life, here are a couple of things you should know:

- It is a process of learning to trust this guidance. In other words, developing your faith. Processes take time. Be patient with yourself.
- Having a gratitude journal is key. I recommend everyone keeps a gratitude journal and writes in it every night. Here's why:
  - At night, we can reflect on our day with gratitude. Be grateful for all doors that opened and for all doors that closed. Trust that the closed doors are guidance too. Marilyn Monroe

"Sometimes good things fall apart so that better things can fall together."
Marilyn Monroe

said, "Sometimes good things fall apart so that better things can fall together."

- o How we go to sleep is how we wake up. Therefore, if you go to sleep happy and grateful, you will wake up happy and grateful.
- o Gratitude raises our vibration, attracts like circumstances into our living experience, and gives us more for which we can be grateful.

- Become more aware of opportunities; these are doors opening for you. Act.
- See everything that doesn't work out for you as guidance to gently nudge you in another direction.
- Ask for guidance proactively, whenever you have a decision to make or feel you are at a crossroads.
    - o Ask with full faith, knowing that you will be guided.
    - o Do not be attached to the outcome, and trust the process.

    > "Gratitude in advance is the most powerful, creative force in the universe."
    > Neale Donald Walsch

    - o Express gratitude in advance that Source will guide you. Neale Donald Walsch says, "Gratitude in advance is the most powerful, creative force in the universe."
    - o Be aware of signs, events, and occurrences that are in response to your asking; surrender to whatever is showing up, and be grateful for it.

CHAPTER 6

Living with Faith

When you start living a guided life, proactively ask for guidance, trust that guidance, and surrender to it, you develop faith, just like a bodybuilder develops a muscle. Using this same analogy, you know that bodybuilders develop strong, defined muscles over time. It's a lengthy process that takes commitment, perseverance, and consistency. It is the same with faith. Faith is cultivated. It is a state of mind. Faith is complete trust or confidence in someone or something. Remember: faith is not belief without proof; it's trust without reservation.

As you develop faith, opportunities show up that will test this faith, and these become defining moments in your life. That was certainly the case for me.

In December of 2013, I was working in my corporate job, doing well and feeling on top of my game in my role because I was using my Silva techniques, getting impressive results, and this made me feel quite empowered. The more I practiced meditating and visualising, the easier things would flow, and I could connect the dots between what I was manifesting and how I was programming my mind. It was at this time that I felt ready to create a new vision for my life. I knew that adding value to others gave my life purpose, and this was something I wanted to do for the rest of my life.

For the first time in over twenty years, I considered leaving the corporate world to work for myself. I was inspired by the idea of adding value to others through speaking, training, and coaching; however, I didn't know how to do that. I didn't know *how* to go from here to there, as I mentioned earlier. I didn't know what that golden bridge out of corporate looked like, and to be very honest, it was scary. The thought of it was quite daunting. There's was that little voice in my head: *You can't do that. How will you pay your bills? There is no way you can just leave your job and start on your own.* I was filled with limiting beliefs about changing direction at forty-three years of age and following my dream.

For the first time in my life, I challenged my limiting belief. I took a stand and said no. Why? It wasn't just a desire; it was an all-consuming passion, a true calling.

Once I discovered what gave my life purpose, the vision of what my dream life could be started to take form. Even so, I didn't know how to go from here to there. So I decided to apply what I believed worked when it comes to manifesting the life you desire.

Step 1: Be crystal clear about what it is that you really want.

So I wrote out a dream statement, my personal vision statement:

> I am so happy and grateful now that I am in perfect health and can work flexible working hours, from any location, doing what I absolutely love to do, doing creative and fulfilling work, with less work and more time to enjoy my hobbies like property, music, boating, travelling, and enjoying fun and laughter with loved ones, friends, and family earning

$____ [I put three times my annual salary at the time].

Step 2: Create a new belief. (This means overwriting my limiting belief that I'm not good enough or will not make enough money doing what I love.) The words of Henry Ford rang loud in my head: "Whether you believe you can or believe you can't, either way you'll be right."

> "Whether you believe you can or believe you can't, either way you'll be right."
> Henry Ford

Creating a new belief requires reprogramming the subconscious mind, and the most effective way of doing this is going into a deep meditative state; visualise living this life, in every detail, until you become emotionally engaged with it. Most importantly were the feelings associated with that visualisation, as if that was already my life.

Hence, with this burning desire to be a speaker, trainer, and coach, and the limiting belief of not knowing how I was going to get there, I stuck to a routine of meditating and visualising almost daily.

A year passed. It was December 2014, and nothing had changed. I looked at my vision statement on my vision board and asked myself why I hadn't manifested this yet. I was still in my corporate job a year later. Then suddenly, and it was intuition, I remembered something I had read by Jack Canfield about the thirty-day principle.

The Thirty-Day Principle

NASA had astronauts wear concave lens goggles 24/7, even when they slept or showered, and this caused them to see the world upside down and back-to-front. The purpose was to see how they'd react to being disorientated in space and whether they would get sick, nauseous, or hostile. After twenty-five to thirty days, however, the astronauts' sight automatically turned right-side up, even though they had been looking at everything upside down. Nobody expected this to happen. This study showed neuroscientists that it takes about thirty days to create a new neuropathway. They redid the experiment with two groups of astronauts; the second group removed the goggles for one day only, on day fifteen. They discovered it took an additional twenty-five to thirty days for the second group of astronauts' sight to correct the image. This proves that it takes at least thirty days, without missing one day, to change a belief, create a new habit, or create a new neuropathway.

After thirty days, your brain will do three different things: Firstly, the part of the brain that controls your perception, the reticular activating system (RAS), will start perceiving resources that you never noticed before. Secondly, your brain will start to sense creative solutions; you'll wake up in the middle of the night with an idea or get an aha moment while you're relaxing or driving. Thirdly, visualising tricks the subconscious mind into thinking that you've already done it.

I realised that I probably did not review my vision board and visualise my vision *every* single day, so I decided to do my own experiment. I opened my notes app in my phone, and every morning after I did my vision visualisation, I typed the date in my phone. This was to make sure I did not miss a day. To my surprise, I missed a visualisation on day eighteen. So what did I do? I started again. The second time around, I missed a visualisation on day twenty-four. What did I do? Started again.

When I eventually crossed the thirty-day threshold, I decided to keep going. At around about this time, I caught up with a friend for coffee and told them, with great excitement, about all the leadership talks and Mastermind classes I was running.

This friend, not knowing my plans to leave corporate at this stage, said to me, "Jeanine, when you talk about leadership and training, your eyes light up. You're on fire. You get so passionate. Why don't you leave your corporate job and do this for yourself as a business?"

I smiled and answered, "I'd love to; that's my dream. I just need to find that golden bridge out of corporate, some form of reliable income to sustain me while I grow the business. I don't know what that is yet, but I know the right thing will just show up. I believe God knows what's in my heart, and I am confident the right thing for me will just show up."

As I said those words, I realised they just came out my mouth, and I believed them wholeheartedly. It struck me that I had created a new belief using the thirty-day principle. This was faith, the belief that it would manifest.

Four weeks later, my golden bridge did show up, better than expected. It was then that I had that flash of intuitive insight when I got that aha idea to call Mike (who sells investment property), and it was during that conversation that he gave me the God-sent opportunity to work for myself as an independent property consultant. The thirty-day principle works, and faith can be cultivated. Faith is about believing. You don't know *how* it will happen, but you know it *will*.

Wayne Dyer wrote a book called *You'll See It When You Believe It*. This is so true. Most people first want to see it before they believe it. However, the universe doesn't give us what we want; it gives us what we believe.

Living with faith is a progression and a practice. You increase your faith as you deliberately and consciously trust it more and more. When I used the thirty-day principle to develop faith, this was done using the will, and a daily discipline of visualising. However, now I live from a place of faith, trusting the signs that show up when I ask for guidance. This is very different and asks more from you in terms of giving up your own agenda and going with the flow. It is moving from fear to faith, from control to surrender.

To illustrate this, let me share the incredible journey of finding office premises. On December 26, 2017, before leaving for a ten-day silent meditation retreat in New Zealand, I asked Nancy, my assistant, to book the venue for the upcoming Silva Method classes that would start mid-February 2018. I got in contact with her around mid-January, only to find out that the venue I wanted to use for the training was booked out for months. Nancy, who I must add is also a divine appointment and like my personal guardian angel, called me in New Zealand and confidently suggested we find our own commercial premises and offer the training there.

This was like a month away from the Silva training; I was gobsmacked that she even thought this feat would be possible. She insisted we look at premises as soon I get back, so I agreed. Nancy went ahead and started to shortlist some commercial properties while I was on holiday. As a backup plan, I provisionally reserved another venue that I'd used many times, even though it was quite expensive, as time was of the essence.

Two days after I landed back in Sydney, Nancy and I had three appointments to view commercial properties. The first one we viewed was in the most ideal location, less than two kilometres from where I live. Wow. After we met the agent and walked towards the door, I noticed it was number 3. I'm not into numerology; however, I have some awareness around numbers, and I know that 3 is a spiritually significant number. I looked it up and found this meaning at first glance: "The appearance of this number is a sign from the angels who are trying to get your attention. They want you to know that your prayers have been heard and that you need to have faith in the divine that your goals and dreams will be manifested in your life."

We walked around this empty office space that had uncarpeted concrete floors, a brand-new bathroom, and a newly renovated little kitchen. The space was ideal in size, large enough for office desks, plus sufficient space for a training room. There was wonderful natural light, as there were windows on both sides; good, natural light was a non-negotiable requirement for me.

As we looked around inside, Nancy (who is very intuitive) immediately said, "This place just feels right and has a great vibe." She tried to persuade me that this was perfect. I, on the other hand, decided to be most logical and use my head to evaluate the space and not get caught up in how the place felt.

When I asked for the price, the premises were $20,000 more than my budget, and almost double of what I expected to pay. All scenarios of what I could do with an extra $20,000 went through my head. I could hire someone else a few days a week. I could invest in more marketing. $20,000 seemed way out of the expected budget, and this made me struggle to enjoy the office that had so much going for it. My logical mind was doubtful that the price met the criteria. Then, whilst in doubt, a few clear and undeniable signs got my attention:

- The agent was Italian (I am too), and his surname translated means "miracle"; The owner's wife's name translated means "Grace."
- Nancy asked me to look at the wall behind me and asked me what I thought it looked like. I had just launched a new website a few weeks prior, and the home page (that I was very particular in choosing) was my photo against a backdrop of white wood panels running vertically. I turned around to look at the wall, and that wall was also made of white wood panels running vertically. It looked like my webpage. How uncanny. All along, I was still trying to remain objective.
- I looked outside the window, and the first number plate I saw was "ME 911." 911 is a highly spiritual number that

encourages you to pursue your life purpose and soul mission as a light worker. This really caught my attention.

- As we walked to the car, a white feather landed between my feet, just outside the premises. We both noticed it and together shouted, "Oh, my God, it's a sign."

- As I approached the car door, this white feather flew up and over my head and stayed right in front of me, somehow pressed against the window in front of my nose, as if the breeze were just holding it there in front of me. By this time, Nancy and I were convinced these were signs from invisible angels.

- Whilst driving to the next commercial property to view, I decided to look up the number 103, which is the street address of this unit. The first reference I read on my phone said this: "Angel Number 103 is a call to attention and your angels remind you that 'everything happens for a reason.' Things are taking place in your life that will set you on a new course of action and/or direction, and the angels ask that you follow as guided as this will be the right path for you. The promptings of your angels and your inner-self will ensure that you take the most appropriate and right action at the right divine time. Listen to the messages of your intuition and inner-wisdom and look out for directions and/or signs from your angels, the ascended masters and universal energies.

"Angel Number 103 is a message from your angels that you are to pay attention to and follow your intuition as you are receiving information and guidance as to the decisions and choices to make and the next steps to take. You are being led towards your divine life purpose and soul mission, and your angels ask that you remain positive and optimistic about your passion/s and purpose. Trust that you have all the skills, talents and abilities within you that are needed to accomplish your goals and aspirations. The angels will ensure that all falls into place for you when you follow their guidance."

All the premises we viewed after that particular one were unsuitable, which left us with a very obvious choice. Of course, for me, cost of the rent was the one thing that was not in favour of signing the lease immediately. We also estimated it would cost $5,000 to $6,000 to furnish it for the Silva training that was now two weeks away. I discussed the dilemma with Nancy and said I would view some more properties before committing to taking the first unit. Nancy agreed, as I had to make the final decision, seeing as I was paying for it.

The next morning, during my Kriya Yoga practice, I asked God in prayer, "Please guide me; please give me an indication if I should take Unit 3 of 103 Majors Bay Road. I don't know what to do. I trust you, Father."

As clear as a voice in my left ear, I heard these words: "How many more signs do you want?"

I was so surprised by this response. It was not what I was expecting, yet I heard it loud and clear. Just like a voice. Then I relaxed and let all the signs of the previous day run through my mind, and it was rather uncanny, I had to admit. This was a defining moment for me. I realised I could either surrender and trust this guidance with full faith or not. It is black and white. I remember thinking of faith as being on one side of a line. I could either stand on the faith side of the line or not. There was no in between.

At that moment, tears rolled down my face, and I thanked God for guiding me and for always taking care of me. I trusted that once again, I would be taken care of, and somehow the money would work out. I thanked God in advance, believing that the money would come and for answering so clearly. I decided that if I truly had full faith, then I wouldn't view any more properties. Looking at other properties would say to the universe, "I don't trust your guidance. I just have to make sure for myself as I am in control." I made my decision. No more viewings.

Walking back to my bedroom to get showered and dressed for the day, I decided to pick up my angel cards just for fun. This seemed like an appropriate time, I thought, with a smile on my face. As I was shuffling, one card jumped out the pack.

The card read "Thank you for guiding my finances so that I can easily afford to pay my rent, mortgage, or taxes."

In the booklet, under the specific meanings, it read "A financial windfall helps you pay your rent or mortgage." Wow, this could not have been clearer.

I opened my emails to scan them, and there was an email from the property office alerting me that I was due $26,000 by invoice: the exact amount for the extra $20,000 a year, plus the cost to furnish it. I burst into tears with heartfelt gratitude for the blessings that had been bestowed upon me that morning.

I went over to Nancy's house, and my first announcement was that I decided not to view any more properties. To my surprise, she shrieked with excitement, jumped with joy, and gave me the biggest hug.

I thought, *Wow, no caution from her to cover my bases. Just another confirmation that this was right.*

When I discussed the sequence of events, some others said that I would have gotten that request to invoice for $26,000 anyway. That money was due to me from selling properties. Yes, I agree; however, it is the timing that is so significant and the uncanny coincidence of the amount of $26,000, which is exactly what I needed to furnish the place and the shortfall in the budget for the annual rent.

The night before signing the lease, I had these words repeating in my head: "This will change also. This will change also." I started to pray and asked what that meant for me. I then had a vision, like a lucid dream, of about twenty spirit guides, angels, and my passed-on loved ones cheering me on, celebrating, and telling me to only focus on the words, "How can I serve?" They reassured me that everything was already taken care of. I intuitively knew this meant that my financial obligations would be met. I said a prayer of thanks, having faith that everything would be taken care of and already is. The next day, I invoiced the property office for another $12,000.

Faith is the power principle of all time.

In the Bible, when the woman touched Jesus and was healed, Jesus turned to her and said, "It was your faith that made you well." Jesus never said that he healed her; he said it was her *faith* that made her well. Faith is the most powerful change agent. It is necessary to cultivate it, and over time, as you learn to trust Source more, you start to live from a place of trust and perpetual gratitude. That is full faith.

There was another divine intervention: Two of the clients who booked for the February Silva training asked to move the training one week later. I asked the others, and they all agreed the later date was preferable for them too. This allowed us enough time to furnish the place and fully kit it out, ready for training seventeen days later instead of ten. Another blessing.

A few months after moving into the new offices, I had an extra Silva class coming up; I added it to the schedule just a few weeks prior at short notice, to give parents the opportunity to graduate in case they wanted to send their child to Silva KIDS, a new programme I launched at the end of April (before a child can attend Silva KIDS, at least one parent must be a Silva Method graduate). Three days before the class, I only had one booking. That morning, during my Kriya Yoga meditation, I asked God to give me a clear sign as to whether I should cancel this class and move the booking to May, or run it regardless. I repeated that I wanted a very clear sign to make sure I didn't misinterpret the answer. That very same day, two new bookings paid for the class and confirmed. If you believe in signs, you receive them. If the direction is right for you and for others, doors will open.

In the middle of April, I received an email from my accountant, reminding me that my quarterly tax return (Business Activity Statement, or BAS) was due at the end of the month. The next morning, during meditation, I remembered that I needed to complete my BAS and pay my tax bill. At that moment, my old conditioning kicked in and caused me to get slightly anxious about having enough money to pay the tax bill. With awareness, I immediately repeated these words over and over till I calmed down and found inner peace: "Thank you, Father, that I can easily afford to pay my mortgages, taxes, and rent. This was your promise to me, and I trust you fully." Later that day, I got an email from the property office to invoice for $16,000.

> "Faith isn't a feeling. It's a choice to trust God even when the road ahead seems uncertain."
> Dave Willis

During the four-day Silva Method class that same April, on the third day, I thought to myself, *This is my first Silva training without a sign that Giammi is present or aware of the work I'm doing. Maybe he is in a higher place and no longer near this earthly plane.*

Whilst thinking this thought, I also somehow wished I would receive some sign that he was with me and around during my classes, like always.

The next day, one of my students sent me a text message saying she would be late, as she must run a quick errand. An hour later, she arrived with a bouquet of flowers for me, and a card she wrote.

The first words she said to me as she walked in the door were, "These flowers are for you from your angel brother. He wants you to know he is always with you." Tears just welled up in my eyes and hers. My heart was bursting with love, and I was overwhelmed with sentiment.

She told me that the previous night, before going to sleep, she had a vision of what exactly happened that day. When she woke up, she felt compelled to honour that vision and get the flowers for me from Giammi. I was blown away. I asked for a sign, and I sure did get one. That was loud and clear. The card read "Your brother never leave[s] you, he is with you! Watching you every day Jeanine. Your brother and God is with you. You are not alone Jeanine," and the reverse side of the card read "Dear Jeanine, thank you for making it possible. You've touched and changed my life and others' lives! Your brother in heaven is very proud to you Jeanine."

When it comes to living with faith, here are a couple of things you should know:

- Desire + belief + expectancy = faith.
- Cultivating faith takes time. It is a process. Be patient with yourself, and start with small steps.

- Initially, focus on creating a new belief by visualising daily for more than thirty days. As you manifest your desire, celebrate and connect the dots that the manifestation is a result of your new belief.

- As you become more confident with your belief and expectancy, trust that Source is from where *all* things come. Have this awareness constantly, and give thanks in advance of your manifestation. Measure your faith by your results. Everything is feedback.

- Create a daily practice of repeating these words in meditation: "I am your humble child. I surrender." With repetition, you will become more humble, which is necessary to release control and have a spirit of teachability. Realise that you are learning to have faith. It is just like developing a new skill, except you must let go of control, not increase it. Saying that you surrender daily starts to marinate in your subconscious mind, and with awareness, you can give up your own agenda slowly but surely, until you practice letting go and start living with faith every day.

- When you ask for guidance, signs, or support and believe you'll get them all, you surely do.

- Living with faith minimises stress because you give up trying to control things.

- If you have faith, let go of your own logic and agenda; the universe rises to meet you.

- If you let go and let God, perfection unfolds, even if it doesn't seem so at the time. Remember that closed doors are also guidance, always for your higher good.

- Living with faith is acceptance. Acceptance is peace of mind.

CHAPTER 7

Living in the Flow

Living in the flow is living like water. Flowing. Moving with the current. Going with the flow of life itself. It is the absence of friction and resistance. It is easy-going. If you could live like water, you too would live in the flow. How does this translate into your life?

When you have an awareness of your constant connection to Source energy, find your life's purpose, and live in alignment with that purpose, whilst accessing your guiding intuition, you are in the flow. You are guided, just like a stream is guided. All streams flow downward to the sea.

You know you are in the flow state when it feels as though the universe has your back, when everything is working out for you. Serendipitous synchronicities are a regular occurrence. On every level, you feel connected, aligned, and in harmony with yourself, with God, and with everything that exists. Physically, you feel energised, healthy, and full of vitality. Emotionally, you feel grateful, supported, loved, guided, and favoured. You feel loving and in accord with whatever you are doing. Mentally, you feel alert, sharp, and focused; you have a real sense of clarity. Spiritually, you feel a genuine connection and alignment with Source. You feel light, weightless, pure, positive, and good. Socially, you are charismatic, attractive, easy-going, and at your best.

Living in the flow is living in alignment, alignment with your values and with God. Living in alignment with your values is often underestimated. Any relationship you have with anything outside of you, that is not in alignment with your values, will come to an end. It is just a matter of time. People with the same values stay together. When people's values are different, whether that's at work, with friends, or with your partner, the relationship will come to an end at some point. What are your values? Are they honesty, integrity, freedom, fun, family, personal growth, loyalty, privacy, openness or hard work? The list goes on.

Living in alignment with your values and with God is a prerequisite for living in the flow, and when you are, it is so pleasant and enjoyable. You feel that loving presence inside your chest, inside your heart space, and always around you, wherever you go. It feels as though this relationship with God is personal, not distant and conceptual, but *personal*. The signs you get when you ask for guidance are so personal, they are overwhelming at times, because it is so clear that this omnipotent, almighty presence is fully aware of you and your every thought, your every emotion, your every action, and your every result. You revel in this wonderful experience of knowing that Source is aware of your every move and helping you every step of the way in your life's journey.

The signs increase in frequency and intensity to remind you of this constant awareness of yourself. Signs that you don't even ask for are just reminders of this very up-close and personal relationship with Source that is beautiful, loving, supportive, and all-knowing. An example would be a thought you have or an insight that comes to you that is helpful, so you think it over or discuss it with a friend. The next day, you get a confirmation of that exact idea or thought from an entity that you highly respect, such as a world-renowned spiritual teacher, a book, or an email from a self-help subscription, or maybe someone shows up to help you further that idea and act on it.

An example would be when I was contemplating developing a kids' programme for the Silva Method. I was thinking about it; however, I had not taken any specific action to make it a reality. A lady who did the Silva Method years prior in Turkey wanted to review the programme, as she was now living in Sydney. She looked up the Silva Method in Australia and found me. This woman also happened to live less than three minutes away from my office and came to meet me after we had a brief conversation on the phone. She was looking to review the four-day programme and said she would not have been able to do so if I was in any of the previous locations I used; she was so happy I now had offices in this particular location. This happened within a month of moving into the new office space, which was really a delightful confirmation that this was right place, right time.

When she came to the office, she mentioned her daughter would benefit from doing the course, as well. This led us down the path of a conversation about Silva KIDS. She got excited and asked about the dates. I did not have any yet; it was just an idea up to that point. I had not even developed the content. Thank God for this lady, who pushed me gently in that meeting for a date when her daughter could attend Silva KIDS. In a most helpful way, considering school holidays and parents' typical agendas, she helped me lock in a date for my first kids' programme. When I mentioned that at least one parent needed to be a Silva graduate for a child to do the Silva Method, she helped me choose dates a few weeks prior to the kids' class to run an extra course for the parents. After our meeting, I added two more Silva Classes to the annual calendar, and from there, everything fell into place, effortlessly.

Living in the flow is a cascade of continuous events, circumstances, serendipitous synchronicities, coincidences, conversations, and extraordinary people who continuously affirm the thoughts you are having and guide you lovingly and specifically in a way that you know is meant for you. It feels as if the world revolves around you, not in the egocentric sense, but rather in the blessed and most loving sense. In the same way, when you go out of your way to please someone you fall in love with, the universe seems to go out of its way to please, love, guide, and support you on all levels.

A big part of living in the flow is *trusting* this flow, having faith, surrendering. I often heard the term *surrender*, and intellectually, I could explain it. I understood it, and I even believed that I was doing it, to a degree. I really had no idea what true surrender really meant, until I read a book that created a sequence of events that changed my life significantly.

A friend recommended I read Michael A. Singer's *The Surrender Experiment*. I could not put this book down. Not only was it the most captivating book, but it also made me realise that I now could understand, at a whole new level, what it means to surrender. It is a true story about Singer's life and how he devoted himself to this lifelong experiment of surrendering and saying yes to life, no matter what showed up. The story is phenomenal. I also found it very intriguing, as I was silently experimenting in my own life with surrendering and trusting that the universe knows what's best for me.

Singer mentioned another book that changed his life: *The Autobiography of a Yogi* by Paramahansa Yogananda, and I immediately bought it too. This book changed my life in the most profound and meaningful way. When I read *Autobiography of a Yogi*, I realised that everything I thought I knew was so far short of a bigger reality. With all that I had read and studied, I realised how little I really knew, especially in the realm of human potential and the myriad miracle workers walking this planet and the astounding things they have accomplished.

In the story of Yogananda's life, he is initiated into Kriya Yoga. As I read about Kriya, I became more and more drawn to it, not out of curiosity, but out of the yearning to come to know God at a deeper and more experiential way. Within a month of finishing the book, I myself went to get initiated into Kriya Yoga. In simple terms, Kriya Yoga is a scientific technique to develop God consciousness. This changed my life and my spiritual awareness forever. Every single day, my life improved more and more. Everything flowed easily and effortlessly. I felt different inside in a way that I've never felt before. I had such a heightened awareness of my aliveness. I was aware of the life force in me that was sustaining me. I was aware of the breath of God breathing me. I became aware that the tingling sensation in meditation is God, manifested in my living, breathing body, and that I really am not controlling it or keeping it alive. My body is a miracle of God's creation that I live inside, with a consciousness and a mind that has infinite potential. I felt my God-manifested-power to heal this body from any dis-ease; without it, I make it unwell, purely with my emotional state that either enhances the divine flow of well-being or interferes with it.

Either way, my body's intelligence was clearly a constant reminder of the God-presence operating in my every cell. The energy life force in every atom of my being was the expression of this God presence. It was through Kriya that I developed this very *personal* relationship with God, as described earlier. Every day, after starting to practice Kriya, I had so many miracles flow into my life. Nothing was a coincidence; everything was divinely guided. I experienced the satisfaction of living in the flow.

Living in the flow doesn't mean that every day is problem free and perfect. It means that when things happen that I don't expect, I trust that this is always for my higher good. It means that I have something to learn, and it's because better things are coming together. I accept it. I welcome it. I have an awareness that even when things don't work out for me, it is to create a new desire for better, which is all perfectly part of my growth and expansion. The new desire keeps me focused, and with gratitude in my heart and faith that everything is always working out for me, synchronicities continue to surprise and delight me, and I am always reminded that I am truly very blessed. I get back in the stream of life, surrender with full faith that the universe supports me in every way as I live with more freedom, fun, and enchantment that comes from living in the flow.

When it comes to living in the flow, here are a couple of things you should know:

- Referring back to the Venn diagram, living in the flow is the sweet spot of the convergence of your three highest priorities:
    - developing a consistent connection with Source
    - finding your life purpose
    - developing your intuition

  This, in turn, opens the way to

    - living on purpose,
    - living a guided life, and
    - living with faith.

  When all these six conditions exist simultaneously, life become magical, wonder-full, joyous, fulfilling, rewarding, meaningful, miraculous, easy, fun, synchronistic, blessed, free, supportive, positive, favourable, and rich.

- Living in the flow and keeping that flow going does not happen by accident. It takes awareness, intentional action, faith, purpose, listening to your intuition, and going with the flow. Going with the flow is saying yes to things that come your way, trusting in the direction of the flow, even when it seems different from your own agenda, your own thought-out path, or your own timing.

- An open mind and an open heart to say yes can only exist when you step forward each day in full faith that some intelligence in this universe is steering you. Letting go of control is probably the most challenging change required. Faith takes practise.

- Living in the flow is when you consciously opt in for living a life that is God's will. This thought scares some people. They think it will take away all their fun and make them live a life of service; they don't want to sacrifice and give up their freedom and what they love. This could not be further from the truth. God is all-knowing, all-powerful, and omnificent; everything, and I mean *every* thing, that could ever exist in your world to bring you your ultimate human experience and open doors for you to live your best life as the grandest version of yourself, could not be better orchestrated for you than by this infinite, loving power that created this entire infinitely intelligent universe.

- Living in the flow requires you to surrender every day and ask God with intent, "May thy will be done." Unless you actually ask God for His will to be done in your life and to guide you to fulfil your highest purpose, you will be left with your own *free* will. This means no intervention without your consent. We all come into this human experience with free will. However, only when you deliberately ask for His will to be done do you summon universal Source energy's unlimited power and presence in your life, which will, no doubt, deliver more to you than you could ever begin to imagine. It will guide you gently and lovingly to fulfil your every dream with purpose, give your life significant meaning, which will, as a consequence, bring about unlimited happiness, belonging, and love in your life.

PART 2

Living beyond Yourself

Why are you here? What are you meant to do here in this short span of human years on this planet? Have you ever really contemplated this question? Think about it, right now. I'd like you to actually stop reading for at least five minutes, close your eyes (this helps you focus better, as 85 percent of your brain's stimulus comes from your eyesight), and ask yourself seriously, why am I actually here? What is the purpose of my life? Please do this now before reading further.

Thank you if you took the time to do that quick exercise of contemplating your own existence.

Either something came up for you, or it didn't. Perhaps it caused a whole lot more questions to be raised. Either way, can you see how fundamental it is to know why you are here? Otherwise, this is all a waste of time, really. You are often so busy making plans and living your lives that you often neglect to contemplate this question at a deeper level. The time when this question probably means the most is at the end of your life, before you pass on, and we *all* will pass on. Therefore, imagine for a minute that you were nearing the end of your life and had to prepare for your departure from this world. What would really bring you a sense of peace and serenity inside and allow you to let go with a sense of satisfaction that you had lived fully? Would money really matter that much? Would you rather have loved ones around you and friends and family checking up on you? Would all the hours at work that you sacrificed make you satisfied, or would the contribution you made to impact other people's lives give your life more meaning? It's quite obvious when you look at it that way, isn't it? These are important questions to ponder. What would make your life seem like it really mattered? That *you* mattered?

It's pretty clear that purpose is our centre-point of our existence, or we live lost. Until you find and live your purpose, you meander through life, searching for satisfaction and happiness. Once you find your purpose, you have direction, and your life has meaning. Happiness comes and goes, but purpose gives you something to hold on to.

Throughout my twenty years in the corporate world, I had many goals and went after them with determination; however, my why, my purpose, was always someone else's: the corporation's. I had a role in a corporate agenda, and I tried to align my actions with their goals and what I thought was my purpose, and in return, I was getting paid for it. Purpose is different from finding that job that makes you happy. Purpose is less about what you want and more about what you give.

Purpose is using your strengths, talents, and gifts to serve others with all your heart. It gives you something to live for, such as healing sick people, raising your children, improving the health and well-being of others, protecting the environment for future generations to enjoy long after you've gone, adding value to others, making an impact on their lives, saving the planet, teaching, and spreading positive energy and actions. I could go on, but I think you get the point.

The more your purpose relates to others, the more significant your life becomes. Hence, the more you live beyond yourself and your selfish needs and desires, the more significant your life will be.

It took me forty-two years to find my life purpose. Whether you are still searching for yours or whether you already know your purpose, the way to live a purpose-driven life is to create a vision for your life first, as described in chapter 4. Once you have that vision, measure it according to how it relates to others. What is the benefit to others if you achieved that vision? This is a great starting point. Then you can start living with more awareness about your power to change things for the better, with love.

Living beyond yourself helps lift you above the hustle and bustle of daily life. It offers transcendence. Your sense of self and your selfish needs fade away, and you feel connected to a higher purpose, and higher reality. You start to see the world with a greater sense of awe and wonder. Your sense of gratitude increases tremendously. You are humbled by what you can give others, by the difference you can really make, because this highlights your own value and your own potential to do good in this world.

CHAPTER 8

Living Fully by Serving Others

"Success is all about me. Significance is all about
others. Once you've tasted significance, success will
never satisfy you again." —John Maxwell

You know how rewarding it is to do something, no matter how small, that makes an impact on someone else's life. These small moments are the times you remember and the memories you treasure. The reason it feels so good to serve others is because that is your soul's true nature. The nonphysical part of us that is always connected to Source is pure love. When you act in harmony with your true nature, your soul's essence, it feels like joy, bliss, and love. You love yourself in that moment, and that's the good feeling you get.

Serving others is also an act of love, and this is who we truly are, beings of love and light, so when you recognise that love that you are, it changes you permanently, and the doorway widens to greater possibilities of increasing the frequency and impact of your acts

"Success is all about me.
Significance is all about
others. Once you've tasted
significance, success will
never satisfy you again."
John Maxwell

of love. If you stop serving and go back to being selfish, you feel more unfulfilled than before. This is because your spiritual evolution depends on it, and you can't go backwards without feeling the discordance of that, and that is the negative emotion you would feel if you moved further out of alignment with your soul's essence and your soul's purpose.

Some people open their hearts and give of themselves; however, if something goes wrong, and they get hurt, they retract and go back into their shell, only looking out for themselves. It's a form of self-preservation. They may deny they feel worse than before, but they really do, because living with anger, bitterness, or resentment is so far removed from our spiritual natures that it feels so off. The more we serve others and change lives, the better it feels.

A few things you should know about living fully by serving others:

- In John Maxwell's book *Intentional Living*, he explains that everyone has good intentions. You have good intentions, and so do I. However, not everyone has good actions. In fact, few do. This takes intentional *action*. We are all naturally selfish, so giving more of ourselves by serving others takes effort. You need to step outside your comfort zone and be highly intentional with your actions.
- Serving others starts in your own home. Before you pat yourself on the back for how much you are doing for others, first take stock of how you are serving the people in your own family. This is often more difficult to do because of all the baggage you carry in your personal relationships; however, it is where you really need to start. That is true leadership. That is leading by example. When the people closest to you respect you the most, you are a true success.
- Serving others and being significant could start with these simple actions:
  - o A handwritten note of thanks to someone acknowledging what they had done and what that meant to you.

o Letting the people who changed your life for the better, or brought you to a turning-point, know that they did, when they did it, and how. Thank them.

o Taking the lead in opening your heart and forgiving someone who really hurt you, and letting them know. Also, thank them for the experience and what it taught you.

o Give something that you value to someone else in a random act of kindness. Do this often.

o Pay attention to what's happening around you, and offer to help, more often, consistently.

o Stop measuring relationships, meetings, and good days by what you get, and measure them by what you *give*.

o Take the time to tell every member of your family how much they mean to you.

o Arrange a day out just with a family member or friend who is often unappreciated, and do something that they would value. Remember to mention how much you love them and appreciate having them in your life. (Take tissues; you may need them.)

• Reflect on your talents, gifts, and abilities and think about how you can serve your community with those gifts. Volunteer for a good cause, become a member of a club that serves the community, donate your time or talents. It's very rewarding and gives you a sense of contribution, a feeling that you made a difference, and this makes life worth living.

• Tithe. This is a spiritual practice. Give away 10 percent of every dollar you earn. It can be to any cause that you feel strongly about helping: animal conservation, children in need, poor communities, disaster relief, environmental causes, or your place of worship; whatever you feel will make a difference in the world that you will feel good about. Why

10 percent? Well, 10 percent is just that little bit of a stretch. 5 percent is much more comfortable. Think about it. What is 5 percent of what you earn versus 10 percent of what you earn? It will require a lot more discipline. However, giving 10 percent will change you and grow you in a remarkable way. It asks more of you to give 10 percent: more generosity, more selflessness, more faith, and more self-control.

If you can trust in Source, from whom all things come, and have faith that you will always be taken care of (and you will), then giving 10 percent away is a physical demonstration of not only your faith in being provided for but also your abundance. If you give 10 percent away to those in greater need than you, it shows that your cup runneth over, literally, and substantiates that you are so blessed to be able to bless others with your wealth and abundance.

When this topic comes up, people often say they can't afford it. My response is, you'll never be able to afford it as long as you think that way, talk that way, and act that way. It's a belief. It's not true. It's a limiting belief that you hold, regardless of your income, expenses, and situation. Tithing develops an abundance state of mind, and it proves to yourself that you *trust* that more will come, and it is acting in accordance with your faith that allows you to give.

This is why it is deemed a spiritual practice. The more you do it, the better you become at it, and the more you actively change your poverty consciousness to an abundance mindset by actively taking action and blessing others in the process. This is one sure way of attracting more abundance into your life. If you can't and don't help others less fortunate than yourself with the money you earn, then you are saying to the universe that you don't have enough, you are in a state of lack. Whatever you think, feel, and believe, you will receive. Money is a currency; like a current, it flows. If you block the flow like water in a dam, it will become toxic, and you literally block the flow. Water that flows like a river stays pure, and it keeps flowing. Money is just the same. Money is an energy too. It's a manifestation of your mindset. It's an outward measurement of your thinking and feeling when it comes to abundance and prosperity. The universal law of reciprocation, or the law of circulation, says that as you give, so shall you receive. You reap what you sow. Nobody has ever become poor by giving. I'll repeat that: Nobody has ever become poor by giving. In fact, it is the very opposite. If you bless others with what you have, you shall in turn be truly blessed. The more you give, the more you receive. Although this is not the reason you should give, like an ulterior motive. You should give because it is the strongest demonstration and reminder that you are so blessed to have a roof over your head, clothes to wear, food to eat, and that you always have more than enough, and therefore with gratitude in your heart for all that you have, you can give and share with others who need it more than you do and be of service to alleviate suffering and hardship that others are enduring. It will also make you feel good about yourself; it is wonderful to do good deeds.

- If you are reading this and think that *you* could do with more money, then my advice is to give more of the money you have away. Yes: If you want more, give more. Giving with love and an open heart of gratitude sends out your vibration and message to the universe that you are wealthy, blessed, fortunate, prosperous, and abundant, and if you practice that feeling, that is what you will get. This is not my opinion; this is the law of attraction, and it applies with precision every single time, regardless of any beliefs or opinions about it. It is consistent; that's why it's called a law. When you raise your awareness and intentionally live in harmony with these laws, life becomes easier, less stressful, and more fun, and you yourself feel more empowered because you know, understand, and practise creating your own reality. This is living fully and being an intentional creator of your own life and circumstances.

You really do live fully by serving others. If you only exist for yourself and your immediate family, then there really is no greater reason for your existence. If you live to give, serve, and make a difference in the world by solving problems for others, then your life really matters. This is living beyond yourself. This is living fully.

CHAPTER 9

Healing Yourself and Others

We all need healing, to some degree or another. Every one of us has some childhood wounds or some adult hurts that have caused us to close our hearts to protect ourselves. These hurts, whether it is loving too much; being abandoned, betrayed, deceived, rejected, judged, criticised, or humiliated; being totally vulnerable and getting hurt; or being repeatedly disappointed by someone, can cause us to build walls around our heart.

To live a fully rewarding and magnificent life, you need to heal your wounds and open your heart. Why? Because your spiritual evolution depends on it. This is your journey. This is your path. This is the work you have to do in this human experience to progress and advance. Your soul chooses to come into this physical experience specifically for your spiritual growth and evolution. Your soul is love, and you should return to love, in your human experience, with a fully opened heart. For us to teach anyone about love, we need to *be* love.

To be of benefit to anyone, you need to start with yourself, because you cannot give away what you do not have. Or rather, you can only give what you have. You can only give what you are. So if you have anger, resentment, or bitterness inside, no matter how long you may have suppressed it, you will attract people into your life, nonstop, that bring this out in you. You will attract people who cause these negative emotions to trigger you to give off more anger, resentment, and bitterness, because you can only give what you have inside. If you don't have any love, you cannot give love, and this cycle will not change until you learn the lesson and heal yourself. People wonder why toxic people are in their lives or their relationships always turn out disappointing. The truth is because they are a vibrational match to what they receive. People outside of you are only a reflection of what's going on inside of you. Every person or situation is a reflection of your vibration, the vibration you broadcast, or what you feel inside emotionally (whether you're aware of it or not).

Life is really a mirror of what is happening inside you. People don't like to hear this and remark that they are not toxic, they are not judgemental, and they are not unreliable, so why are they attracting these kinds of people into their lives? The answer is because somewhere, somehow, they are doing this to themselves. You may not be all those negative characteristics to others; however, somewhere in your own life, you are treating *yourself* this way. So if you have people who judge you, where in your life are you judging yourself? If people let you down and cannot be trusted, where in your life do you let yourself down? Where can't you trust yourself? If people break promises to you, where do you break promises with yourself? Can you see that everything is a reflection of what is going on inside yourself? I love this, even though it can be very confrontational. I love it because all the clues as to where and how we need to heal ourselves are all around us. People are our mirrors. Relationships show you what you need to heal. It all starts with you. It all starts with self-love.

Self-love and self-appreciation are the keys to opening your heart and healing your wounds. People often complicate life and think they need months or years of therapy or counselling to make advancements and heal their wounds. This is not necessarily so. Start actively practising self-love, and you will make significant progress in a short space of time. Just start.

Your behaviour (lack of self-love, for example) is driven by your subconscious programming, or your paradigm. If you don't love yourself, it shows in your behaviour. This can be how you treat your body, how you take care of your health, how you treat other people, how you treat animals, how much you invest in your personal development, how satisfied you are with your job, how much time you spend doing what you love, and how much you are loved by others. All these experiences are a measurement of self-love.

Therefore, in order to change your behaviour, you need to change your programming. In other words, you need to change the beliefs and attitudes you hold about yourself, and you need to change your habits. The easiest way to do this is to work at the foundation: the subconscious mind. Habits and beliefs are in your subconscious mind. Of course, you could work on your behaviour straight up, using will power and effort; however, that is usually not sustainable, and you eventually revert to your old behaviour unless you change your programming. You need to change your self-image, the image you hold in your mind of who you are, and love that person more. This is why suddenly changing habits and changing behaviours is so difficult. Think of fitness as a good example, or meditating daily. If it was so easy to suddenly change behaviours, we would all be skinny, fit, rich yogis. Changing behaviour permanently requires changing your programming, and then it all flows effortlessly from there.

Changes, or what I call impressions on the subconscious mind, require two things: repetition and emotion. That's why people use affirmations or mantras; it is the repetition that makes an impression on the subconscious mind over time. Emotions, on the other hand, are much more effective and make stronger impressions on the subconscious mind. How do you just generate emotions? You do this by using visualisation, mental rehearsal, or dynamic meditation.

If you can visualise loving yourself more, seeing yourself approving of yourself, appreciating yourself, being proud of yourself, and then feeling the happy emotions associated with that imagery, you can change your self-image and develop more self-love. At the same time, you need to act in the outer world in harmony with your intention to love yourself more. The outward action needs to be congruent with the inside action.

The more you love yourself, the more inclined you are to opening your heart. The more you open your heart; the more love can flow to you and through you. God is love, and the more open your heart is, the more of this divine, infinite love can flow through you, not only healing you but others as well.

The more you love yourself, the more aligned you are with your true nature, the more aligned you are with your soul, and the more you love yourself, the more you can love others, and your love, especially unconditional love, can make others stronger, more courageous, and heal them too. You heal them because being loved is healing, and also because you lead by example. The best way to teach others is through who you are, and by your own actions. You can and should all live with the intention to help others through your own example.

Very often, one of the key steps towards self-love is self-forgiveness. As much as you hold things against people who hurt you, you tend to be much harder on yourself and, more often than not, very unforgiving with yourself. Just like loving others, forgiving others also starts with yourself. You can

> "Happiness cannot be found from physical or external conditions such as wealth, power, or bodily pleasure, but from living a life that is right for your soul, your deepest good."
> Socrates

forgive yourself for present and past choices you made. You cannot change the past, and having regrets only stores negative emotions inside yourself, which over time can damage your health and reduce your ability to manifest more goodness, abundance, love, and joy in your life. Every emotion you hold, whether active or supressed, affects your vibration, which determines what you manifest into your life. Therefore, the better you feel, the better you live. Getting rid of stored anger, resentment, hate, and bitterness is a *requirement* to live your best life and allow all that you dream of to flow into your experience. It starts with yourself and your relationship with yourself; your self-love and self-forgiveness. This is the pathway to opening your heart and loving others, healing others and forgiving others.

This is freedom. Freedom to love without reservation, to be open to all of life, to give copiously, to contribute purposefully, to make this world a better place and, therefore, live fully. This is when you find true happiness. Socrates said that "happiness cannot be found from physical or external conditions such as wealth, power, or bodily pleasure, but from living a life that is right for your soul, your deepest good." This is so true. Happiness is not a goal, or something you find or chase. Happiness is something you *are*, as a result of what you give, far more than a result of what you get. Giving is love. Giving is the nature of your soul.

In a more literal sense, you can also heal yourselves, physically, from poor health. The Silva Method teaches specific techniques to heal yourself from all and any conditions. This is done in dynamic meditation at the alpha level, using visualisation and mental rehearsal. These techniques are extremely effective and have cured people I personally know from conditions ranging from insomnia to full body paralysis, including headaches, diabetes, epilepsy, arthritis, and even cancer. The Silva Method also teaches how to heal others. Science today has thankfully acknowledged remote healing, energy healing, and prayer healing, whatever name you wish to give it. The statistics provide undeniable proof that it works. This technique is one of the greatest gifts you can give another person: to heal them, with or without their knowledge.

This is love. This is truly living beyond yourself. In his extraordinary book *Silva Mind Control*, José Silva tells a story that illustrates the power we have if we allow Source to flow through us to serve others. José got a university to verify his research on his work with remote healing. They said if he could get ten cases to work on, where people had conditions they were not expected to recover from, and he could heal two, that would be statistically significant. If only one healed, that could be by chance; however, two would prove it works.

José worked these cases without these people's knowledge, so that there would no possibility of it being psychosomatic or the power of suggestion. Over a three-year period, all ten were healed. This is astounding. Why am I sharing this with you? Because you can do this too. Yes, you can. Jesus said, "More than this you can do," when he performed miracles. We all have the potential to focus this infinite energy from Source and do wonderful, miraculous work. Reiki, energy healing, and prayer healing are all examples of healing by proxy, focusing this omnipotent energy. When you take the time to improve your awareness, knowledge, and skills to heal yourself and then extend this benefit to heal others, you'll see the transformation taking place; there is nothing more gratifying and rewarding. This is living fully. This is healing, not only the person, and you, but it heals the planet too, and your example can inspire someone else to do the same. One person can make such a difference in this world. That person is you. You can make a difference, change a life, improve conditions on this planet, and heal yourself and others. You can make your life worth living, a life with meaning, a life that matters, a life that you're proud of, and a life that inspires those around you to become better.

A few things you should know about healing yourself and others:

- The formula for healing yourself is a lot simpler than we make it out to be. Love yourself. This is the starting point. Love yourself. Forgive yourself. Heal yourself. Open your heart.

Forgive others. Heal others. Heal the world.

- Loving yourself requires active steps; it is not automatic. Firstly, become aware of and elevate your own self-love and appreciation; it's only in that feeling place where you can allow all your dreams and goals to manifest in your life. There's no other way. You only get what you think you deserve, and you only believe that you are worthy and deserving, depending on the relationship you have with yourself and how much self-appreciation and self-love you actually demonstrate. Here are three tips:

  o 1. Self-Awareness

     Become really aware of how you feel about yourself. Say to yourself, in your mind or out loud, "I love myself." How did that feel? Did it feel uncomfortable, or did you really feel good about the idea that you do love yourself? Either way, you will have a knowing and an awareness of where this relationship is and how much work on self-love you need to do. Self-awareness is being aware of your self-talk every day; understand whether it's positive or negative. What kind of things are you saying to yourself? Are they good, loving, affirming, and encouraging? If not, if you run yourself down or call yourself stupid or bad names, just say, "Cancel, cancel," and overwrite that with a positive affirmation. Do this continuously, and be intentional about moving towards more self-love and appreciation, one thought at a time. This technique is from the Silva Method and is probably one of the most underestimated skills. Neuroscience has proven that you are programmed by everything you say to yourself in your mind. The brain takes everything literally. Negative self-talk can affect performance, as can positive self-talk. Each time you say something negative to yourself, you create a neuropathway. This becomes stronger with repetition, until it becomes a habit and then your belief. How you speak to yourself is a habit; all of us have negative self-talk to some degree or another. The "Cancel, Cancel" technique may seem simplistic, yet it is highly effective. It stops the negative neuropathway and overwrites it with your positive affirmation, which is the new neuropathway. Each time you do this, you program yourself positively, which enhances performance, and over time, this becomes your new habit of positive self-talk and ultimately a new belief. The more you love yourself, the more you heal and the greater your capacity to love others, heal others, and show others the way through leading by example.

o   2. Unconditional Self-Love

It's very easy to love yourself when you have done something good, or when you have achieved some goal in your life. However, to love yourself and appreciate yourself without conditions is the highest form of self-love. The days you make mistakes or make poor choices, you have the opportunity to change the story. Change what you say to yourself. Appreciate yourself more. Say something like this: "Yes, I made a mistake, but this is how I learn. I appreciate and love myself for being open to making mistakes because this is how I acquire more skills and more knowledge to better myself for my future." Or, "I really messed up today, but I love myself for being okay with that. I love myself for being easy about making mistakes or messing things up because it gives me an opportunity to try it again and do better next time." Eliminate any self-talk that puts you down. Practise using "Cancel, Cancel" and then a positive affirmation to overwrite it, and over time, you will love yourself more. The most important voice to listen to is your own. Make sure it's positive and encouraging.

o 3. Practise Makes Improvement

What do you practise? Whatever you practise, you get good at. Louise Hay taught me so much about developing self-love, and she always advocated mirror work. I tried it and have to say it does work. There is something incredibly powerful about looking yourself in the eye and talking to yourself. I strongly encourage you to practise this affirmation for the next thirty days: stand in front of the mirror, look yourself in the eye, and say, "I love myself. I believe in myself, and I am worthy and deserving of fulfilling all of my desires." If the thought of this makes you feel even a bit uncomfortable, you need this the most. Say it twenty times in the morning and at night. This will absolutely change your self-image. Your self-love, confidence, and self-esteem will be elevated.

This is guaranteed. Whatever you tell yourself, your subconscious mind takes in and believes. I once met a man who came from very challenging circumstances and had a rough start in life. He got up in front of an audience and told his story with confidence, excitement, and enthusiasm. He bought himself a click counter and held it up in his hand. He proudly announced that he had told himself he loves himself over three hundred thousand times. This had changed his life. He encouraged all of us to live our dreams and gave an impromptu motivational speech about the value of affirming that we love ourselves. I never forgot this.

- When it comes to forgiveness, whether that is self-forgiveness or forgiveness of others, you need to remind yourself that it is a spiritual practice. It's not a one-time exercise, and all is forgiven. You need to practise forgiveness, and over time, you become better at it. It is something that you do repeatedly, with the intention to let that issue go,

> "Holding on to anger is like drinking poison and expecting the other person to die."
> Buddha

knowing it is in the past, which you cannot change, and acknowledging that it is interfering in your present, which is creating your future. Getting started is always the part that meets with most resistance. Why? Why do we resist forgiveness? I heard it once said that it is because we haven't finished punishing the person. This seems so illogical when put that way; however, this is why we can't let go. Somehow, holding on to the anger feels like we are getting the person back in some way. Yet it only hurts us. Buddha said that "holding on to anger is like drinking poison and expecting the other person to die." The other person is unaffected by our anger and resentment. This is why forgiveness is probably the greatest gift you can give yourself, because it opens your heart and heals you. Mark Twain said that "forgiveness is the fragrance that the violet sheds on the heel that has crushed it." That is so beautiful.

- Forgiveness is a spiritual energy and changes us the more we practise. I'm sure you have heard this saying before: "To err is human; to forgive, divine." It brings us into alignment with our soul and increases our capacity to love one another.

- Some tips on helping to forgive others:
  o Put yourself in the other person's shoes. Try to understand their past. A person cannot give away what's not inside of them. People who are full of pain, inflict pain on others. This may help you see the world through their eyes, which leads to compassion.
  o If you *really* knew what they were going through, you would understand that they are doing the best they can, from *their* level of awareness at the time. I am also talking about people who do terribly violent things, violate the rights of others, commit terrible crimes, whatever it may be. They are doing the best from *their* level of awareness, and their circumstances have brought them to that level of awareness. This may not sound like something you want to hear, or something that you even want to believe, but this is the truth.
  o Forgiveness is not an act of condoning someone's behaviour if they have hurt you or done you wrong. It has less to do with the perpetrator and more to do with freeing *yourself* from the past, which is holding you back from enjoying more love, better health, prosperity, and happiness, because these

positive outcomes can never come from any kind of negative emotion.

- Make a list of those who have hurt you. Actively, deliberately, and intentionally forgive anyone who has done you wrong.

> "Forgiveness is the fragrance that the violet sheds on the heel that has crushed it."
> Mark Twain

- Writing a letter to the person may also be helpful. The intention is to burn it afterwards (not send it) to release that from your energy and from your past. Express gratitude to the person for giving you the experience and acknowledge what it taught you. If you learned from it, it served a valuable purpose.
- When it comes to health and healing yourself and others, and if this inspires you, or makes you even curious, take the next step. Make enquiries. Take a course. Read a book. Do the Silva Method; there are classes all over the world. Just take the next step. This will make a significant difference in your own life and the life of others.

CHAPTER 10

Living Your Legacy

"We will continue to take part in constructive and creative activities, to make this a better world to live in, so that when we move on, we shall have left behind a better world for those who follow."

—José Silva

I remember the most difficult exercise I ever had to do on self-development was when I first joined the John Maxwell Team, and we were studying the book *The 21 Irrefutable Laws of Leadership*. I was asked to write my own obituary. I had to put down on paper what people would say at my funeral. What would I be remembered for? It's one thing to think about it, but it is by far something else when having to actually do it. I really struggled with it. The reason was that at the time, when I was still working in a corporate job, I had such a desire to make a bigger impact in the world, yet I didn't know *how* or *what* specifically I could do to make a significant difference. The only thing I did know was that I wanted to add value to others and help them be more successful. I could not see the big picture; however, I knew that speaking, training, and coaching on leadership and self-development were my absolute passions. I had also already experienced the joy and satisfaction of living this passion, even though back then, it was in a small way, one Mastermind class at a time, sometimes just one person at a time. This gave me a sense of purpose, and once I had a purpose, I had hopes, and I could dream. I could dream bigger, and so I did.

My role model was John Maxwell, who had an impact on millions of lives; he trained millions of leaders who are making a difference all over the world, and so I knew what living a life of significance looked like. I had big dreams; I just had to start.

The reason writing one's own obituary was challenging was because most people *accept* their lives; they don't create their lives intentionally. They don't take the lead and initiate. However, if you look throughout history, the greatest change-agents and the greatest leaders have been those who were intentional about making a difference; they went out and made it. They never waited for the right conditions and circumstances; they never waited for a lucky break, a better economy, or a better partner, employee, or spouse. They went out, took action, and believed in themselves and in their purpose.

In my own life, once I had taken the time to write out my obituary, I got a greater sense of determination and clarity of purpose. I never knew *how* I would make the transition from my corporate role to speaking, training, and coaching; however, what I did know was that by hook or by crook, I would make it happen. Somehow, someway, this would be my resolve, my commitment to myself, so that when I pass on, I would have no regrets. I kept telling myself I would rather die trying than live with regret. Whatever it took, I was prepared to give it my best shot.

> "If one advances confidently in the direction of his dreams, and endeavours to live the life which he has imagined, he will meet with success unexpected in common hours."
> Henry David Thoreau

Once the mind becomes clear and focused, and your emotions are charged with passion and determination, it is amazing how the universe conspires to make things happen for you. Henry David Thoreau said, "If one advances confidently in the direction of his dreams, and endeavours to live the life which he has imagined, he will meet with success unexpected in common hours."

I love the phrase "if one *advances*." Just keep advancing. Just take the next step. You don't need to know the entire route, the whole plan; just take the next step. Maxwell always said that when he gave his first talk, only two people showed up, and one was his wife, Margaret. Today, he can easily fill a stadium of a hundred thousand people. The point is that he started somewhere from very modest and unglamorous beginnings. Everybody does. Just take the next step and keep moving forward in the direction you want to go.

A legacy is also a story. What story are you telling about yourself? When you meet someone new, pay attention to the story you tell about yourself. What do you say, and how do you say it? This is so important. It helps you understand how you became you. We are the authors of our stories, and we can change how we tell them.

Your life is not just a list of events. You can evaluate, interpret, and learn from every single event. For example, I could say, "My life was good, then my brother passed on, and it became bad, and I've never recovered from the loss. It saddens me every day." On the other hand, I can tell this story: "My life was good; however, it lacked *purpose*, and I was so focused on my own goals and achievements that I could not see it. Losing my younger brother at just twenty-one made me take stock of my own life. The tragedy helped me realise I wanted *my* life to count. I wanted to make a difference and live my best life so that if I passed on suddenly, I would be happy with my life, knowing it mattered, and I made a difference. This helped me find my life purpose, and since then, my life has got better and better, and I live each day with gratitude and fulfilment, knowing that I'm doing what I love and making a difference in the world."

We can all change our story by reflection and evaluation, and we should. Socrates said that "the unexamined life is a life not worth living." This is so true. Experience does not teach us anything; it is just

> "The unexamined life is
> a life not worth living."
> Socrates

an experience. However, *evaluated* experience is a great teacher. We have all had pain in our lives and some form of suffering. Embracing painful experiences by learning from them through reflection and evaluation can lead us to new insights and wisdom.

When I was working in the corporate world, public speaking was part of my role. I was fortunate to have done a lot of public speaking in my life, and it was an area I was confident in, so I offered to coach and mentor people after hours, for free. Training was always my passion, and I loved it. After several weeks, I decided to join Toastmasters to get feedback and improve my speaking further. After just two weeks at Toastmasters, I was so inspired, I decided to start a Toastmasters Corporate Club at work. I had the specific intention of helping those I was mentoring in a more formal way and offering a wider reach. With the help from long-standing Toastmaster members, and the agreement from management at work to subsidise the fees for members, it got set up in only a few weeks. It took off with great success, and I had the pleasure of observing people learn, grow, and significantly improve their public speaking and their confidence. The club still exists today after several years and will continue for years to come. This is a legacy. It may not be huge, have an impact on millions, or change the world; however, it does leave a place where you've been in a better condition than when you found it.

What can you do? What can you create? What can you start that will benefit others and go on long after your departure?

There are a few things you need to know when it comes to living your legacy:

- With these two ingredients, you can live your legacy:
  - o know your purpose
  - o live a life of significance, which is all about serving others

- The best advice and suggestion comes from John Maxwell, who says, "One day someone will summarise your life in one sentence. Pick yours now!" Take the time to pick *your* sentence. This will give you the greatest sense of clarity. It is also the bullseye of the dartboard for your life. Without a clear target, where will you aim?
- You don't need to be world famous, powerful, or highly influential to start living your legacy now. Sometimes the simplest deeds, when done with love and the sincere intention to add value, have the greatest impact. The greatest compliments I get are from people who worked for me years ago (some for just a few months), when they contact me to tell me a story about something I said to them, or something I taught them all those years ago, that changed their life. This is legacy.
- Legacy is multiplied when you add value to others with the intention of instilling in that person the desire to continue to add value to others, as you did to them, but without you, and with the understanding for them to pass this on, as they continue to pay it forward, and so on. This is true leadership. It is not just developing followers but developing leaders who will develop and raise up more leaders.
- Legacy starts with a mindset to leave a place or person in a better condition than you found them.

The most important time for humanity is now. Our planet is at a critical tipping point, and humanity requires a lot more change in a lot more people for us to survive and thrive as a species. It requires you to make a difference. You are already fully resourced. Nothing needs to be added to you to make a significant difference in this world.

The only hope for a better world resides in your ability to develop more love and compassion for human beings, animals, and plants. The only thing that keeps us going, that gives us strength to carry on, to survive, is love.

> "We will continue to take part in constructive and creative activities, to make this a better world to live in, so that when we move on, we shall have left behind a better world for those who follow."
> José Silva

All the knowledge and the wisdom in the world will never transform lives and make this world a better place to live in. It requires love and compassion. It requires you to find your purpose in this world, to start living it today with intention and serving with your whole heart. It requires you to be determined to be part of the transformation to make this a better world, not the problem. It's too late to turn a blind eye with the awareness you have now. It's irresponsible to sit on the fence, watch, and wait. You are brave, courageous, and able to be the hero in your own story. Be the one who does what it right, not what is easy. Living your legacy starts now.

In the words of Shah Rukh Khan:

"The future-you needs to love others in order not to perish with its own self-absorption, otherwise it will cease to flourish.

You can use your power to build walls and lock them out, or to break them down and welcome them in.

You can use your faith to make people afraid and terrify them to submission, or you can use it to give courage to the people so they can rise to the greatest height of enlightenment.

You can use your knowledge to create nuclear bombs or you can use it to spread the joy of Light to millions."

Living beyond yourself is not just a choice, it is a necessity. There is no coincidence that you are reading this. The world needs you and the expression of the talents and gifts you've been blessed with; otherwise, you are depriving the world of your unique and valuable contribution. My friends, let your light shine.

Let Your Light Shine
Marianne Williamson

Our deepest fear is not that we are inadequate.
Our deepest fear is that we are powerful beyond measure.
It is our light, not our darkness, that most frightens us.
We ask ourselves, who am I to be brilliant,
gorgeous, talented, fabulous?
Actually, who are you not to be?
You are a child of God. Your playing
small does not serve the world.
And as we let our own light shine, we unconsciously
give other people permission to do the same.
As we are liberated from our own fear, our
presence automatically liberates others.

Printed in the United States
By Bookmasters